MW01115623

Author: One Exam Prep (1-877-804-3959)
www.1examprep.com

ABOUT 1 EXAM PREP

1 EXAM PREP TAKES PRIDE IN BEING THE MOST EFFECTIVE AND EFFICIENT EXAM PREPARATION SCHOOL IN THE INDUSTRY.

All of our Classes and Exam Prep Material is available 24 Hours a Day online when you purchase a online course at **www.1examprep.com** or call 1-877-804-3959 **Access** the **information** whenever and as often as you need.

No Classrooms

No Time Schedules

No Pressure

We provide the TOOLS for YOU to be SUCCESSFUL on YOUR schedule, not ours!

ALL of the Information you need is available at ONE LOW PRICE!

We provide you with exactly what you need to be successful. We are up to date with ALL of our Textbooks. No Bait and switch. No hidden upsells. We invite you to compare......

WE HAVE THE LOWEST TEXT BOOK PRICES IN THE INDUSTRY!!!!!

1 Exam Prep takes pride in our students and in their success. We want you to pass your exam the first time, every time in the most cost efficient way. We offer the most comprehensive, easy to follow, **easy** to use **exam preparation** techniques in the industry. We offer both State and County Licensing Exam Prep Courses throughout the United States. We have helped thousands of students successfully pass State and County Licensing Exams and we are seriously committed in helping you!

ALL OF OUR COURSES INCLUDE OUR PROVEN 4 POINT LEARNING SYSTEM UNRIVALED IN THE INDUSTRY YOU WILL RECEIVE:

TABBING AND HIGHLIGHTING INSTRUCTIONS

The most comprehensive, up to date Tabbing and Highlighting instructions found anywhere in the industry. Our experienced instructors will provide you with more tabs, more highlights than any other exam prep school in the country. We know the material cover to cover. We show you what you need to know and where you will find it, when the pressure is on and the clock is moving.

TEST TAKING TECHNIQUES

Learn the strategy on how to be the most efficient and effective on exam day. Learn how to manage the exam, the questions and the clock and make it work to your advantage

PRACTICE QUESTIONS AND ANSWERS

We provide our students with 1000's of Questions and Answers to help you prepare for your exam. We are continually updating and adding relevant questions with answers to prepare for the current exams. Our years of experience and thorough knowledge of the subject matter and testing formats allow us to provide you with the skills needed to address each question on the exam.

TEXTBOOK OVERVIEW

You will receive a high level summary on each textbook you receive and is required for your exam. The summary will outline the topics covered in the textbook, where these topics can be in the textbook and the types of questions most likely to be answered in each textbook. You will also learn which parts of the textbook and which questions are aimed at a particular trade(s). Being thorough, efficient and confident is a huge advantage on exam day. Our Textbook Overview will help you manage your time and efficiency when the pressure is on and you need to stay focused.

TABLE OF CONTENTS

Testing Company Info

Below is the testing company information you will need concerning your exam.

EFFECTIVE IMMEDIATELY!

ALL BROWARD COUNTY EXAMS REQUIRE A 75% CORRECT TO PASS, NOT 70%

If you need any assistance or have questions please email **support@1examprep.com**

If you are having problems opening the pdf links to practice tests, highlights & tabs, and answers. you may have to update your adobe reader.

Gainesville Independent Testing Service, LLC

Examinations Engineered To Your Needs

Ocala Office:
1644 NE 22ND Ave Suite E
Ocala, FL 34470
P.O. Box 831127
Ocala, FL 34483-1127
Open Monday - Friday 8am - 4:45pm
1-800-997-2129
1-352-369-GITS (4487)
Fax: 1-352-387-2443

GITSLLC.org Testing FAQ's

We at GITS are constantly striving to provide you with the most current items and references. The date of publication on some of our reference books may not be the most recent edition of that book. What that means is that the MAJORITY of items from that book come from that edition/version. If you buy a newer version of the book it will contain the material needed to reference items on your test, but it will also contain some information the the groups of Licensed Subject Matter Experts for the field of work being tested on have not yet approved items for use on the examinations. You are free to use any edition/version from the one listed to the current.

NEW TESTING LOCATION!

North West Corner of Palmetto Park Road & Powerline Road in Boca Raton

Broward/Palm Beach Office
7025 Beracasa Way Suite #107A
Boca Raton, FL 33433

Scheduling

There are two simple ways to schedule your examination:

Call Toll Free (800) 997-2129
E-mail your contact information to gitsllc@gitsllc.net and we will call you as soon as we receive your information.

Please have a Government issued ID and a Visa, Mastercard or Discover Card available when you are ready to schedule an appointment. Payment is due when appointment is made.

Cancellation/Rescheduling

To cancel an examination you must contact us with a minimum of 5 Business days (Monday- Friday, except Holidays.) To reschedule you must contact us no later than 24 hours (1 full day) prior to your scheduled date. Multiple rescheduling MAY result in an additional fee to cover administrative cost.

Florida Testing Rates

Below is the list of Florida testing rates

2 Hour Exams: $80
3 Hour Exams: $100
4 Hour Exams: $120
Exams in Spanish: $25 extra
Electronic Testing: $50 extra
Reviews: $40

Scope

Flooring Category--Class "FL": The scope of work of a Class "FL" specialty building contractor shall include and be limited to the fabrication and application of floor surface materials made of asphalt, vinyl, sheet vinyl, cork linoleum, parquet wood, wood strips, and similar pre-finished surface flooring materials which are prefabricated or cast-in-place. A Class "FL" specialty building contractor may also repair, paint, and relay resilient tile floor coverings. In order to be eligible to be certified as a Class "FL" specialty building contractor by the board, the applicant shall have at least one (1) year of practical experience in the category.

Examination Outline

The Flooring Contractor--Class "FL" examination is based on trade-specific information pertaining to materials, tools, equipment, practices, terminology, and relevant laws. The examination is a two (2) hour, open book exam that consists of 50 questions.

Open Book

Total Questions
Time limit:

50
2 hours

Correct required to pass   70% - 75% Depending on Your County

Exam Specs

Subjects	No. of Items
Safety	8
Wood Strip Flooring	11
Parquet and Patterned Flooring	7
Substrate	7
Sheet Vinyl Flooring	7
Estimating and Plan Reading	10
Total Questions: 50	

Approved References

Florida Building Code (Building), 2017
Code of Federal Regulations – Title 29, Part 1926(OSHA)
Carpentry and Building Construction, 2010

Test Taking 101

Read each question carefully and read all the answers before you make a selection. Once you choose the answer to a question, look it up in the reference books. This is especially important even if you believe you know the answer without looking it up. Examination questions are validated by state codes and reference books, not merely according to standard practice. By answering a question solely by experience, you could unknowingly give an incorrect answer. Although experience is helpful, it is still to your benefit to look up each answer.

Sample
Question: The
sky is _____.

Blue

Green

Red Orange

If the reference book says that the sky is green, guess what the correct answer to the question the sky is green. If you mark blue, you are wrong for not following the directions of finding the correct answer in the book.

This is not a test of what you know, this is a text of problem-solving techniques. The State or County has research that has proven that all good business owners

MUST have problem-solving skills. If they do not possess these skills, they
have 4 times more of a chance of going out of business.

For best performance, go through the examination several times.

On the first pass, answer all the easy questions and write what book(s) (and chapter)
you
think the answer will be in.

On the second pass, take one book at a time and go from the front to the
back of each book, by chapter, and answer the questions in the most efficient
manner.

On each successive pass of the test, you will find the harder questions:

DO NOT SPEND 5 MINUTES ON A QUESTION UNTIL THE END OF THE TEST.

ALL MATH QUESTIONS ARE ATTEMPTED LAST.

DO NOT LEAVE ANY ANSWERS UNANSWERED. TAKE OU BEST GUESS, YOU
WILL HAVE A 25% CHANCE OF GUESSING CORRECTLY. Many of my students
have passed the test on this method only.

4. Relax, take a 30 second- or 1-minute break every 30-45 mins.

You do not have to answer any of the very hard questions to pass the test. Learn to identify them early in the process, skip them and take 25% at the end.

Most people think that they have 2 minutes and 24 seconds per question (120 mins / 50 questions) . Where if you do not attempt the very hard questions, you will have 3 mins and 10 seconds per question (120 minutes / questions).

Cross out the question on your test after you have found the correct answer.

This will ensure that you do not waste any time rereading a question that you have already answered, thus wasting your most valuable asset….. TIME!

Important Tip: If you are taking a paper and pencil exam, place a small check mark on the answer sheet next to any question you are going to skip.

This will do two things for you:

1.Reserve the answer line of the questions you are skipping

Instantly tell you which questions you need to look at again

Only one answer is right. If two answers mean the same thing, then they are both wrong. - Use scratch paper for math computations and work neatly. Place the number of the question next to the computation, and draw a line to separate it from the rest of your work. That way, if you decide to go back and check your answers, you can easily find your math for a question.

Do not use your scratch paper as an answer sheet. Some candidates number down the side of the scratch paper, record their answers there and then transcribe them onto the answer sheet later. This practice is time-consuming and increases the risk of error. Even worse, some candidates do not remember to transcribe their answers and turn in blank answer sheets!

Remember: only the answer sheet will be scored.

o Your final score will be determined from the answers you record on the answer sheet. Allow time to record an answer for each question, but **DO NOT** mark more than one answer per question. After the time is called, no further marking of the answer sheet will be allowed. If you are unsure of an answer, it may be better to guess, since you will **NOT** receive credit for any question left blank. Select the closest or best answer for each question.

If you want to change an answer, make sure before you do so that you have clearly made an error and have seen the mistake. Then, erase carefully and completely.

When you have finished the examination, take a close look at your answer sheet. Check each line to make sure there is only one answer marked for each question and that you have completely erased any changes, check marks, or stray lines. Candidates taking computer-based tests may scroll back through the test to review and change answers if necessary.

After you finish the examination, raise your hand and wait for the examiner to check your papers for completeness before leaving your seat. You may then leave the room.

Filling Out Your Answer Sheet

For Paper and Pencil testing, you will be given a scan-able answer sheet and will be asked to bubble in your answers to each question. You may also be asked to bubble in some additional information such as your name, social security number, and the test number that is printed on your test booklet. You may be asked to sign a statement that you will comply with the test administration rules, procedures, and guidelines and that you will not divulge the test questions.

For computer-based testing, you will be using a keyboard and/or a mouse to enter your response to each question. You will be given time and a tutorial to familiarize yourself with using the keyboard or mouse to select your answers. If you complete your test and have time remaining, you will be able to review any or all questions and change your responses. You may also be asked to indicate agreement with a statement that you will comply with the test administration rules, procedures, and guidelines and that you will not divulge the test questions. (LOL)

STRATEGIES FOR TAKING A STATE OR COUNTY EXAM

The amount of time spent studying is not the only factor in being prepared. It is also very important to study efficiently. If you want to retain what you are studying, you must set up a system. You are better off if you study for one hour in a quiet, private and relaxed atmosphere than if you study for 15 minutes at a time, 6 or 8 times a day. So, start your exam preparation by setting up a schedule and picking an appropriate area.

Rules to help you study more effectively

Make sure that you know the meaning of words that are unfamiliar to you. Keep a list of the unknown words, look up their definitions and then keep going back to review the list.

Always try to follow your study schedule and plan.

Practice the rules for answering multiple choice questions while you are doing practice questions.

Find your weakest areas and then concentrate your study in those areas.

Write down problem questions and go back over them later. Bring them to the class and ask the instructor to review questions.

Be sure to tab the books and become familiar with the tabs, indexes, and table of contents so you can find things quickly.

Time yourself, so you know how long you are spending on each question.

The Test Day

Remind yourself how well you will do on the exam.

Get a good night's rest. Get up early and remind yourself how well you will do on the exam. Eat a good breakfast. Remind yourself how well you will do on the exam.

Be sure to wear comfortable clothes. Wear or bring a sweater that you can add or remove depending on the room temperature. Remind yourself how well you will do on the exam.

Get to the exam site early. If you have to rush to find the site or get to the room, you may not do as well on the exam. Remind yourself how well you will do on the exam.

Don't get nervous or excited. Remember, if all else fails, there is always another day.

General rules to answer multiple choice questions

Read the directions carefully and be sure that you understand them.

Look over the answer sheet and be sure you understand how to mark your answers.

Be carefully when transferring answers from the test to the answer sheet. Be sure to:

Mark answer completely,

Only mark one answer per question,

Make no extra marks on the answer sheet,

If you make an error, erase,

Be sure to mark the answer in the correct spot on the answer sheet. Repeat the answer to yourself as you transfer it to the answer sheet. And then check it again on the test sheet, repeating it.

Read the question carefully and be sure you understand what it is asking. Cross out any extraneous information. Read the question again.

Read all the answers before you make a choice. Quite often a "possible" answer is listed before the correct answer. **Don't be caught by this trap.**

Eliminate all choices that are wrong choices. After you read all the answers then cross out the wrong answers and chose from the remaining.

Never pick an answer because of a pattern to the answers on previous questions. There is no pattern. Just pick the answer you feel is correct.

Be aware of key words that may help select an answer. Absolute words, such as: always, never, only, all or none. These words usually indicate an incorrect answer. Limiting words such as: some, many, most, sometimes, usually, normally, occasionally, will often indicate the correct answer.

Skip over a question that gives you trouble or is taking too long to solve. Mark it in the question book so you can find it later. Continue through the exam and come back to the question after you are completed. Be sure to save five minutes at the end of the test period, so that if there are any unanswered questions, you can at least guess at the answer.

10. Never leave a question unanswered. There is no penalty for a wrong answer.

Watch for negative question, such as, "Which of the following would make the statement false?"

12. How to make an educated guess. If there are four choices, you have a 25% chance to pick the correct answer. But you may be able to improve those odds.

Eliminate the incorrect answers.

Look for answers with absolute or limiting words.

Look for answers with obviously the wrong sign (+ or -).

Look for two answers with the same meaning, they are probably both wrong.

Look for two answers with the opposite meaning, one of them may be correct.

If all else fails and you must guess, always guess the same choice.

13. Be careful changing answers. Remember that your first guess is normally the best. If you have time at the end of the exam you should go back through the test. But, only change answers if you are sure that your first choice is incorrect, *i.e.* you find a calculation error.

GOOD LUCK. Remember to keep reminding yourself that you will do fine and pass the exam!

If you have no confidence in yourself, you are twice defeated in the race of life. With confidence you have won before you've started-----MARCUS GARVEY

There are 24 hours in a day. If 8 of them are spent sleeping, that gives you 16 hours to get some efficient and productive study done, right? It seems simple enough. There are plenty of hours in a day, so why is it so hard to use this time effectively, especially around exam time? We've found that managing their time effectively is one of the things that students struggle the most with around exam time. However, time management is also one of the things that schools never teach – how frustrating?!

In the weeks leading up to study leave, every teacher you have for every class you go to seems to pile on the work: Mrs. Gibb from English class tells you that you have to prepare 3 practice essays for both your visual and written texts, your Geography teacher Miss Wood expects you to do every past exam paper for the last three years before the exam, Mr. West your Math teacher says that you have to finish all of the questions in that darned AME textbook if you want to do well on the exam.

But they expect you to do all of this without giving you any time management tips. Mrs. Gibb, Miss Wood and Mr. West all fail to tell you how it's humanly possible to complete all this work without collapsing when you walk into the exam hall. **That's where we come in!**

Read on for the time management tips that your teachers never gave you!

1. Focus on what you must study – not what you don't.
It seems obvious, but think of all the times you've sat down to study, and you've ended up spending 2 hours studying the concepts you already know like the back of your hand.

It's easier to study the subjects you like. Studying the concepts that you're already confident in is a lot less challenging than studying the concepts that you find the most difficult, as your brain will have to work less to learn this information. Studying what you already know is a bad time management strategy because you'll leave all the important stuff to the last minute meaning you won't have the time to cover these concepts in depth.

The trouble with this tip is that it's often hard to decipher what you know and what you don't.

To figure out what concepts you already know, and what concepts you still need to learn, complete a subject audit. A subject audit involves breaking down a subject into several points or sections and then analyzing how well you know each of these points. You should spend most of your time studying those concepts that you have rated the most difficult.

The key for effective time management is to review the easier material, but allow enough time to cover the harder concepts in depth so you're not left to study all of the most difficult concepts the night before the exam.

2. Work in sprints.

You may think that to have good time management skills you have to spend all your time studying. However, this is a misconception that many students hold.

Think of studying for exams like training for a marathon.

On your first day of training, you wouldn't go out and run 42kms. You would burn- out quickly due to a lack of prior training, and you would probably be put off running for a long time. This would not be a good way to manage your time. The better route to success would be to slowly work up to running the 42kms by running a bit further every day.

This simple idea of training in short bursts has been proven effective in all areas of human performance. You don't have to be a marathon runner to use this strategy!

When studying, you should start out small by studying in short, focused 'sprints' followed by brief breaks. Start by studying in 15- minute bursts followed by one 10 minute break.

Over time, slowly increase the length of time you're studying (and breaking) for.

This strategy is effective because studying for short bursts promotes more intense focus and will give your brain the time to process and consolidate information as opposed to studying for long periods of time which is not effective and may increase your chances of burnout.

Don't think of effective time management as studying for three hours straight with no breaks, think of effective time management as using your time wisely and in ways that will best promote retention of information.

Follow these steps to practice effective time management and become an expert studier (or marathon runner!) in no time:

Set a timer for 15 minutes.

Put in some solid study until the timer goes off, making sure you're spending every minute working with no distractions.

Have a ten-minute break to check your phone, walk around, stretch, get outside etc.

Rinse and repeat.

Increase the amount of time you're studying for as you begin to feel more comfortable studying for extended lengths of time.

Make a study system.

I'm sure you've been lectured by every teacher you've ever had to "make a study plan!!!" Study plans are effective for your time management, however they're sometimes hard to stick to.

Here at Study Time, we find that the 'study system' is an effective strategy for really getting to the root of what you're studying. A study

system is easier to stick to, and therefore fosters better time management
skills, because it breaks tasks down into small chunks.

A study system is basically a simple list of steps that you can make to outline the steps you're going to take when you study. The list should start simple (4-5 things), but over time it should become more complex as you add steps to it.

Just like a workout plan at the gym or for sport, it will give you a clear direction of what action to take, making study much more efficient.

Over time, you can experiment with new study methods, and add them in to optimize the system.

Below is an example study formula that you could use when studying:

Download the "Achievement Standard" from the NCEA website

Turn this into a checklist for what you already know and what you need to know

Break the checklist into main themes using a mind map For each

theme, make a summary sheet

After that, break down the key points of each summary and put

these onto flash cards Read through your notes and ensure you

understand them, and then hit the flash cards

Test yourself on all of them first, then make two piles, one that's

wrong and one that's right. Then redo the wrong pile again

Get someone else to test you

Practice exam papers – test yourself using exam papers from the

past 2-3 years and time yourself

Work through the answers

Write a sheet of all tips/tricks i.e. things you got wrong in the

practice exam papers Redo exam paper and make model answers

Adjust flashcards if necessary, i.e. make new ones based on the

exam papers Re-test all your flashcards

Creating a study system will keep you on track and it will allow you to effectively plan out your time while studying.

4. Practice distributed learning.
Imagine your Math teacher gave you seven equations to do for homework. How would you answer these questions? Would you do one question per day for seven days, or would you do all seven questions in one day?

You may think that it would be a better time management strategy to do all seven questions at once and get them over and done with. However, this is an ineffective way to manage your time.

The brain works better when it has time to process information. Neuroscience has shown that your brain needs time to consolidate information that has been newly learned, in order to form strong links between neurons and thus strong memories.

If the learning is done in one big chunk, you'll just forget it after three days. However,

if you review it a day after, then you'll retain it for seven days.

When making a study schedule, you should space out when you study for each subject. For example, don't spend one day studying
English, then the next day studying Math, then the next day studying Biology.

Instead, you should alternate studying for these subjects throughout the day. Do one hour of Math, then one hour of English study, then one hour of Biology, and so on.

This is a much better way to manage your time, because the more often you review a concept, the more solidified it will be in your mind. This is because there will be more time to consolidate this into your memory. Also, taking breaks between reviewing certain concepts will give your brain time to process the information.

Try it out!

1 Exam Prep
Florida Building Code-Building, 2017
Tabs and Highlights

These 1 Exam Prep Tabs are based on the *Florida Building Code-Building-2017 Edition.*

Each Tabs sheet has five rows of tabs. Start with the first tab at the first row at the top of the page, and proceed down that row placing the tabs at the locations listed below. Place each tab in your book setting it down one notch until you get to the bottom of the page, and then start back at the top again. After you have completed tabbing your book (the last tab is usually the glossary, appendix, or index), then you may start highlighting your book.

1 Exam Prep Tab	Section#
Table of Contents	vii
Asbestos Removal	105.3.6
Inspections	110
Business Group B	304
Allowable Building Heights & Areas	503
Fire-Resistance Rating Requirements	Table 601
Fire Blocking	718.2
Cover Thickness - Reinforced Concrete Floor	Table 722.2.3(1)
Design Occupancy Load	1004.1
Riser Height/ Tread Depth	1011.5.2
Ramps	1012
Guards	1015
Exit Access Travel Distance	1017
Corridor Width	Table 1020.2
Emergency Escape	1030
Ventilation	1203

1 Exam Prep Tab	Section#
Min. Thickness of Weather Coverings	Table 1405.2
Overflow Scuppers	1503.4.2.1
Flashings: Base & Counter	1507.2.9.1
Equipment Clearance	1510.10
HVHZ-Reroofing	1521
Site Grading-Slope	1804.4
Rubble Stone Foundation Walls	1807.1.3
Depth & Width of Footings	1809.4
Deep Foundation	1810
Wall Panels	2002.5
Fireplace Clearance	2111.12
HVHZ - Quality, Tests, & Approvals	2119
HVHZ - Steel Construction	2214
Truss Drawings	2303.4.1.1
Allowable Span – Wood Panel/Subfloor Underlayment	Table 2304.8(4)
Fastening Schedule	Table 2304.10.1
Floor Joist Bearing	2308.4.2.2
Cutting and Notching	2308.5.9
HVHZ - Quality	2315
Hazardous Locations	2406.4
HVHZ	2410
Gypsum: Showers & Closets	2509

1 Exam Prep Tab	Section#
Elevator Accessibility	3009
Coastal Construction Control Line	3109
Protection of Pedestrians	3306
Protection of Adjoining Property	3307

This concludes the tabs for this document. Please continue with the highlights on the following page.

1 Exam Prep Tab	Section#
Elevator Accessibility	3009
Coastal Construction Control Line	3109
Protection of Pedestrians	3306
Protection of Adjoining Property	3307

Section #	Highlight
101.2	**Scope**: The provisions of this code shall apply to the construction, alteration, relocation, enlargement … or any appurtenances connected or attached to such buildings or structures. Highlight exception 1 and 2.
102	**Applicability**
102.1.1	The Florida Building Code does not apply to, and no code enforcement action shall be brought with respect to … or to programmatic requirements that to not pertain to enforcement of the Florida Building Code.
102.2	**Building:** The following buildings, structures, and facilities are exempt from the Florida Building Code … and provided by law: Highlight exemptions (a)-(k).
105	**Permits**
105.1	**Required:** Any owner or authorized agent who intends to construct … shall first make application to the building official and obtain the required permit.
105.1.1	**Annual facility permit:** the building official is authorized to issue an annual permit for any occupancy to facilitate routine …equipment installations/relocations
105.2	**Work exempt from permit:** Highlight: Mechanical; 3. Portable cooling unit
105.2.1	**Emergency Repairs**: the permit application shall be submitted within the next working business day to the building official.
105.3.2	**Time limitation of application:** An application for a permit for any proposed work shall be deemed to have been abandoned 180 days after the filing … not exceeding 90 days each.
105.3.4	A building permit for a single-family residential dwelling must be issued within 30 working days … for processing the application.
105.3.5	**Identification of minimum premium policy:** Workmen's Compensation, every employer shall, as a condition to receiving a building permit, show proof that it has secured compensation for its employees.
105.4	**Conditions of the permit**
105.4.1.3	Work shall be considered to be in active progress when the permit has received an approved inspection within 180 days.
105.7	**Placement of permit:** The building permit or copy shall be kept on the site of the work until the completion of the project.
105.8	**Notice of commencement**: the authority issuing such permit shall print on the face of each permit card in no less than 14-point, capitalized, boldfaced type: "WARNING TO OWNER … BEFORE RECORDING YOUR NOTICE OF COMMENCEMENT."

Section #	Highlight

105.10 — **Certificate of protective treatment for prevention of termites**: A weather-resistant job-site posting board shall be provided ... and another copy for the building permit files.

105.11 — **Notice of termite protection:** A permanent sign which identifies the termite treatment provider ... The sign shall be posted near the water heater or electric panel.

105.12 — **Work starting before permit issuance**: Upon approval of the building official, the scope of work delineated ...and the work does not proceed past the first required inspection.

107 — **Submittal Documents**

107.2 — **Construction Documents:** Construction documents shall be in accordance with Sections 107.2.1 through 107.2.6.

107.2.1 — **Information on Construction Documents:** Construction documents shall be of sufficient clarity to indicate location ... as determined by the building official.

107.3.5 — **Minimum plan review criteria for buildings:** The examination of the documents by the building official shall include the minimum criteria and documents ... and all exterior elevation. Note: Familiarize yourself with all the areas of the plans:
- **Commercial Buildings: Building**
- **Electrical**
- **Plumbing**
- **Mechanical**
- **Gas**
- **Demolition**
- **Residential (one- and two-family)**

Exemptions: Plans examination by the building official shall not be required for the following work: 1 – 6.

109 — **Fees**

109.4 — **Work commencing before permit issuance:** Any person who commences any work on a building, structure, electrical gas ... shall be subject to a fee established by the building official.

110 — **Inspections**

110.8 — **Threshold building.**

110.8.1 — The enforcing agency shall require a special inspector to perform structural inspections ... by the engineer or architect of record.

110.8.2 — The special inspector shall determine that a professional engineer who specializes in shoring design has inspected the shoring ... subject to more than the minimum number of inspections required by the Florida Building Code.

Section #	Highlight
202	**Definitions:** Key definitions include: - Accessible Means of Egress - Aerosol - Atrium - Awning - Basement - Building Line - Common Path of Egress Travel - Dead Load - Floor Area, Gross - Floor Area, Net - Dwelling - Dwelling Unit - Floating Residential Unit - High Velocity Hurricane Zone - Live Load - Live Load, Roof - Material Code Violation - Permanent label - Public Way - Sleeping Unit - Story - Threshold Building
302	**Classification**
302.1	**General**: Where a structure is proposed for a purpose that is not specifically provided for in this code, such structure shall ... according to the fire safety and relative hazard involved. 1. Assembly 2. Business 3. Educational 4. Factory and Industrial 5. High Hazard 6. Institutional 7. Mercantile 8. Residential 9. Storage 10. Utility and Miscellaneous
303	**Assembly Group A**
303.1	**Assembly Group A:** Assembly group A occupancy includes, among others, the use of a building or structure … or drink consumption or awaiting transportation.
303.1.1	**Small buildings and tenant spaces:** A building or tenant space used for assembly purposes with an occupant load of less than 50 persons shall be classified as Group B occupancy.
305	**Educational Group E**

Section #	Highlight
305.1	**Educational Group E:** Educational Group E occupancy includes, among others, the use of a building or structure, or portion thereof, by six or more persons at any time for educational purposes through the 12th grade.
306	**Factory Group F**
306.2	**Moderate-hazard factory industrial, Group F-1:** Factory industrial uses which are not classified as factory industrial F-2 … not be limited to, the following: Highlight: Millwork (sash and door).
306.3	**Low-hazard factory industrial Group F-2:** factory industrial uses that involve the fabrication or manufacturing of noncombustible materials … not be limited to, the following: Highlight: Metal products (fabrication and assembly)
307	**High-hazard Group H**
307.1	**High-hazard Group H:** High-hazard Group H occupancy includes, among others, the use of a building or structure, or portion thereof, that involves the manufacturing … Hazardous occupancies are classified in groups H-1, H-2, H-3, H-4 and H-5
307.1.1	**Exceptions:** The following items shall not be classified as Group H, but shall be classified as the occupancy that it most nearly resembles. Highlight items 1 - 15.
307.1.2	**Hazardous materials:** Hazardous materials in any quantity shall conform to the requirements of this code, including Section 414, and the Florida Fire Prevention Code.
307.3	**High-hazard Group H-1:** Buildings and structures containing materials that pose a detonation hazard shall be classified as group H-1.
307.4	**High-hazard Group H-2:** Buildings and structures containing materials that pose a deflagration hazard or a hazard from accelerated burning shall be classified as Group H-2.
307.5	**High-hazard Group H-3:** Buildings and structures containing materials that readily support combustion or that pose a physical hazard shall be classified as H-3.
307.6	**High-hazard Group H-4:** Building and structures which contain materials that are health hazards shall be classified as group H-4.
307.7	**High-hazard Group H-5:** Semiconductors and comparable research and development areas in which hazardous production materials are used … shall be classified as Group H-5.
307.8	**Multiple Hazards:** Building and structures containing a material or materials representing hazards that are classified in one or more Groups H-1, H-2, H-3, and H-4 shall conform to the code requirements for each of the occupancies so classified.
308	**Institutional Group I**

Section #	Highlight
308.1	**Institutional Group I:** Institutional Group occupancy includes, among others, the use of a building or structure, or a portion thereof, in which care or supervision is provided to persons ... detained for penal or correctional purposes or in which the liberty of the occupants is restricted. .
308.3	**Institutional Group I-1:** This occupancy shall include buildings, structures or portions thereof for more than 16 persons who reside on a 24 hour basis in a supervised environment and receive custodial care.
	This group shall include, but not be limited to, the following: Highlight: Congregate care facilities.
308.4	**Institutional Group I-2**: This occupancy shall include buildings used for medical care on a 24-hour basis for more than five persons who are incapable of self-preservation.
	This group shall include, but not be limited to, the following: Highlight: Psychiatric hospitals
308.5	**Institutional Group I-3:** This occupancy shall include buildings and structures that are inhabited by more than five persons who are under restrain or security.
	This group shall include, but not be limited to: Highlight: Jails
308.5.1	**Condition 1:** This occupancy condition shall include buildings in which free movement allowed ... means of egress without restraint.
308.5.2	**Condition 2:** This occupancy condition shall include buildings in which free movement allowed ... Egress to the exterior is impeded by locked exits.
308.5.3	**Condition 3:** This occupancy condition shall include buildings in which free movement allowed ... means of egress from such a smoke compartment to another smoke compartment.
308.5.4	**Condition 4:** This occupancy condition shall include buildings in which free movement is restricted from an occupied space.
308.5.5	**Condition 5:** This occupancy condition shall include buildings in which free movement is restricted from an occupied space.
309	**Mercantile Group M**
309.1	**Mercantile Group M:** Mercantile Group M occupancy includes, among others, the use of a building or structure or a potion thereof, for the display and sale of merchandise.
	Mercantile occupancies shall include, but not be limited to, the following: Highlight: Drug Stores.

Section #	Highlight

310   **Residential Group R**

310.3   **Residential Group R-1**: Residential occupancies containing sleeping units where the occupants are primarily transient in nature, including:
Highlight: Boarding Houses, Hotels, Motels. Congregate living facilities with 10 or fewer are classified as R-3

310.4   **Residential Group R-2**: Residential occupancies containing sleeping units ... where the occupants are primarily permanent in nature, including:
Highlight: Congregate living facilities with more than 16 occupants

310.5   **Residential Group R-3**: Residential occupancies where the occupants are primarily permanent in nature and not classified as R-1, R-2 or R-4 or I, including:

310.6   **Residential Group R-4**: Residential Group R-4 occupancy shall include buildings, structures or portions thereof for more than five but not more than 16 persons ... The persons receiving care are capable of self-preservation.

311   **Storage Group S**

311.1   **Storage Group S**: Storage Group S occupancy includes, among others, the use of building or structure or a portion thereof for storage that is not classified as hazardous occupancy.

311.2   **Moderate-hazard storage, Group S-1**: Buildings occupied for storage uses that are not classified as Group S-2. Highlight the list under this section.

311.3   **Low-hazard storage, Group S-2:** Storage Group S-2 occupancies nclude, among others, buildings used for the storage of noncombustible material.

Group S-2 storage uses shall include, but not be limited to, storage of the following:
Highlight the list under this section.

312   **Utility and Miscellaneous Group U**

312.1   **General:** Group U shall include, but not be limited to, the following:
Highlight the list under this section.

401.2.1   **Additional design criteria: Scope** — Highlight from Section 449 thru Section 3109

402   **Covered Mall and Open Mall Buildings**

402.1   **Applicability**: The provisions of this section shall apply to buildings or structures ... nor more than three stories above grade plane.

402.7.5   **Fire department access to equipment:** Rooms or areas containing controls for air-conditioning systems ... elements shall be identified for use by the fire department.

Section #	Highlight
403	**High-Rise Buildings**
403.1	**Applicability**
	Exception: The provisions of Sections 403.2 through 403.6 shall not apply to the following buildings and structures: Highlight 1-5.
404	**Atriums**
404.1	**General:** In other than Group H occupancies, and where permitted by Section 712.1.6 … shall apply to buildings or structures containing vertical openings as defined as "Atriums."
406	**Motor-Vehicle Related Occupancies**
406.4	**Public parking garages:** Parking garages other than private parking garage … shall be classified as either an open parking garage or an enclosed parking garage.
406.4.1	**Clear height:** The clear height of each floor level … shall not be less than 7 feet.
406.4.2	**Guards:** Guards serving as vehicle barrier systems shall comply with Section 406.4.3 and 1015.
406.4.3	**Vehicle barriers:** Vehicle barriers not less than 2 feet 9 inches in height shall be placed … below is greater than 1 foot.
406.4.4	**Ramps:** Vehicle ramps shall not be considered as required exists unless pedestrian facilities are provided. Vehicle ramps utilized for vertical circulation as well as for parking shall not exceed a slope of 1:15.
406.5	**Open parking garages**
Table 406.5.4	**Open Parking Garages Area and Height**
410	**Stages, Platforms, and Technical Production Areas**
410.4.1	**Temporary platforms**: Platforms installed for a period of not more than 30 days are permitted to be constructed of any materials permitted by the code.
504	**Building Height and Number of Stories**
505.3.2	**Automatic sprinkler system increase**: shall be fully protected by sprinklers above and below the platform.
506	**Building Area**
506.3	**Frontage increase:** Every building shall adjoin or have access to a public way to receive an area factor based on frontage. Area factor increase shall be determined in accordance with Sections 506.3.1 through 506.3.3.

Section #	Highlight
602	**Construction Classification**
602.2	**Types I and II:** Types I and II construction are those types of construction in which the building elements listed in Table 601 are of non-combustible materials, except as permitted in Section 603 and elsewhere in this code.
602.3	**Type III**: Type III construction are those types of construction in which the exterior walls are of non-combustible materials and the interior building elements are of any material permitted by this code.
602.4	**Type IV:** Type IV construction (Heavy Timber, HT), is that type of construction in which the exterior walls are of non-combustible materials and the interior building elements are of solid or laminated wood without concealed spaces.
Table 602	**Fire-Resistance Rating Requirements for Exterior Walls Based on Fire Separation Distance**
Table 601	**Fire-Resistance Rating Requirements for Building Elements (Hours)**
Table 602.4	**Wood Member Size Equivalencies**
602.5	**Type V:** Type V construction is that type of construction in which the structural elements, exterior walls and interior walls are of any materials permitted by this code.
701.1	**Scope:** The provisions of this chapter shall govern the materials, systems and assemblies used for structural fire resistance-rated construction … safeguard against the spread of fire and smoke within a building and the spread of fire to or from buildings.
705	**Exterior Walls**
705.2	**Projections:** Cornices, eave overhangs, exterior balconies and similar projections extending beyond the exterior wall shall conform to the requirements of this section. Projections shall not extend any closer to the line used to determine the fire separation distance shown in Table 705.2
Table 705.2	**Minimum Distance of Projection**
705.2.1	**Type I and II construction**
705.2.2	**Type II, IV or V construction**
705.2.3	**Combustible projections:** Combustible projections extending to within 5 feet … or where protection of some openings is required shall be of at least 1-hour fire-resistance-rated construction.
Table 705.8	**Maximum Area of Exterior Wall Openings Based on Fire Separation Distance and Degree of Opening Protection**

Section #	Highlight
705.11	**Parapets:** Parapets shall be provided on exterior walls of buildings.
705.11.1	**Parapet construction:** Parapets shall have the same fire-resistance rating as that required for the supporting wall ...shall have non-combustible faces for the uppermost 18 inches, including counter flashing and coping materials.
706	**Fire Walls**
Table 706.4	**Fire Wall Fire-Resistance Ratings**
706.4.1	**Townhouse fire separation**
706.4.1.1	Each townhouse shall be considered a separate building and shall be separated from adjoining townhouses by a party wall complying with Section 706.1.1. Separate exterior walls shall include one of the following: Highlight: 1. A parapet not less than 18 inches above the roof line.
706.5	**Horizontal continuity:** Fire walls shall be continuous from exterior wall to exterior wall and shall extend at least 18 inches beyond the exterior surface of exterior walls.
706.6	**Vertical continuity**: Fire walls shall extend from the foundation to a termination point at least 30 inches above both adjacent roofs.
718	**Concealed Spaces**
718.2.1	**Fire blocking materials**: Fireblocking shall consist of the following materials: Highlight: 1 – 8.
720	**Thermal-and Sound- Insulating Materials**
720.2	**Concealed installation:** Insulating materials, where concealed as installed buildings ... shall have a flame spread index of not more than 25 and a smoke-developed index of not more than 450.
720.3.1	**Attic floors**: Exposed insulation materials on attic floors shall have a critical radiant flux of not less than 0.12 watt per square centimeter when tested in accordance with ASTM E 970.
721	**Prescriptive Fire Resistance**
Table 721.1(1)	**Minimum Protection of Structural Parts Based on Time Periods for Various Noncombustible Insulating Materials**
Table 721.1(2)	**Rated Fire Resistance Periods for Various Walls and Partitions**
Table 721.1(3)	**Minimum Protection for Floor and Roof Systems**
722	**Calculated Fire Resistance**

Section #	Highlight
Table 722.2.1.1	**Minimum Equivalent Thickness of Cast-in-Place or Precast Concrete Walls, Load-Bearing or Nonload-Bearing**
Table 722.6.2(1)	**Time Assigned to Wallboard Membranes**
Table 803.11	**Interior Wall and Ceiling Finish Requirements by Occupancy**
804	**Interior Floor Finish**
804.4.2	**Minimum Critical Radiant Flux:** In all occupancies, interior floor finish and floor covering materials in enclosures for stairways and ramps … The minimum critical radiant flux shall not be less than Class I in groups I-1, I-2, and I-3 and not less than Class II in Groups A, B, E, H, I-4, M, R-1, R-2 and S.
903	**Automatic Sprinkler Systems**
903.3.1.2	**NFPA 13R sprinkler systems:** Automatic sprinkler systems in Group R occupancies up to and including four stories in height shall be permitted to be installed throughout in accordance with NFPA 13R.
1001.2	**Minimum requirements**: It shall be unlawful to alter a building or structure in a manner that will reduce the number of exits or the capacity of the means of egress to less than required by this code.
1003	**General Means of Egress**
1003.2	**Ceiling height:** The means of egress shall have a ceiling height of not less than 7 feet 6 inches. **Exceptions:** Highlight 1-8.
1003.3	**Protruding Objects**
1003.3.1	**Headroom:** Protruding objects are permitted to extend below minimum ceiling height required by Section 1003.2 provided a minimum headroom of 80 inches shall be provided for any walking surface, including walks, corridors, aisles and passageways. **Exception**: Door closers and stops shall not reduce headroom to less than 78 inches.
1003.3.2	**Post-mounted objects:** A free-standing object mounted on a post or pylon shall not overhang that post or pylon more than 4 inches where the lowest point of the leading edge is more than 27 inches and less than 80 inches above the walking surface. **Exception**: These requirements shall not apply to sloping portions of handrails between the top and bottom riser of stairs and above the ramp run.

Section #	Highlight
1003.3.3	**Horizontal projection:** Objects with leading edges more than 27 inches and not more than 80 inches above the floor shall not project horizontally more than 4 inches into the circulation path.
	Exception: Handrails are permitted to protrude 4 1/2 inches from the wall.
1003.5	**Elevation change:** Where changes in elevation of less than 12 inches exist in the means of egress, sloped surfaces shall be used. Where the slope greater than one unit vertical in 20 units horizontal (1:20), ramps complying with Section 1010 shall be used. Where the difference is 6 inches or less, the ramp shall be equipped with either handrails or floor finish materials that contrast with adjacent floor finish materials.
1004	**Occupant Load**
Table 1004.1.2	**Maximum Floor Area Allowances Per Occupant**
1005	**Means of Egress Sizing**
1005.3.1	**Stairways**: The capacity in inches, of means of egress stairways … means of egress capacity factor 0.3 inch per occupant.
1005.3.2	**Other egress components**: The capacity in inches, of means of egress components other than stairways … means of egress capacity factor of 0.2 inch per occupant.
1005.5	**Distribution of egress capacity:** Where more than one exit, or access to more than one exit … not reduce available capacity to less than 50 percent of the required capacity.
1008	**Means of Egress Illumination**
1010	**Doors, Gates, Turnstiles**
1010.1.1	**Size of doors:** The minimum width of each door opening … clear width of 32 inches.
	Means of egress doors in a Group I-2 Occupancy used for the movement of beds shall provide a clear width not less than 41 1/2 inches. The height of door openings shall be not less than 80 inches.
	Exceptions: Highlight 1-10.
1010.1.1.1	**Projections into clear width:** There shall not be projections into the required clear width lower than 34 inches above the floor or ground.
	Exception: Door closers shall be permitted to be 78 inches minimum above the floor.
1010.1.2	**Door swing:** Egress doors shall be of the pivoted or side-hinged swinging type.
	Exceptions: Highlight 1-9
1010.1. 6	**Landings at doors**: Landings shall have a width not less than the width of the stairway or the door, whichever is greater.

Section #	**Highlight**
1010.1.7	**Thresholds**: Thresholds at doorways shall not exceed 3/4 inch in height for sliding doors serving dwelling units or 1/2 inch for other doors.
1010.1.9.2	**Hardware height:** Door handles, pulls, latches, locks and other operating devices shall be installed 34 inches minimum and 48 inches maximum above finished floors.
1011	**Stairways**
1011.1	**Width and capacity**: shall not be less than 44 inches.
1011.3	**Headroom:** Stairways shall have a headroom clearance of not less than 80 inches measured vertically from a line connecting the edge of the nosings.
	Exception: Spiral Stairways complying with Section 1010.10 are permitted a 78-inch headroom clearance.
1011.5.2	**Riser Height and tread depth:** Stair riser heights shall be 7 inches maximum and 4 inches minimum. The riser height shall be measured vertically between the nosings … intersections with the walkline and a minimum tread depth of 10 inches within the clear width of the star.
1011.5.4	**Dimensional uniformity**
	Exceptions: 2. Consistently shaped winders, complying with Section 1009.7, differing from rectangular treads in the same stairway flight.
1011.8	**Vertical rise**: A flight of stairs shall not have a vertical rise greater than 12 feet between floor levels or landings.
1011.10	**Spirals stairways**: Spiral stairways are permitted to be used as a component in means of egress … from a space not more than 250 sq. ft.
	A spiral stairway shall have a 7 ½ minimum clear tread depth at a point 12 inches from the narrow edge …. The minimum stairway clear width at and below the handrail shall be 26 inches.
1011.11	**Handrails**: Stairways shall have handrails on each side and shall comply with Section 1014. Where glass is used to provide the handrail, the handrail shall also comply with Section 2407.
1011.12	**Stairway to roof:** In buildings four stories or more above the grade plane, one stairway shall extend to the roof surface, unless the roof has a slope greater than 4:12.
1012	**Ramps**
1012.2	**Slope**: Ramps used as part of a means of egress shall have a running slope not steeper than one vertical unit in 12 horizontal units. The slope of other pedestrian ramps shall not be steeper than one unit vertical in eight units horizontal (12.5-percent slope).

Section #	Highlight
1012.3	**Cross slope:** The slope measured perpendicular to the direction of travel of a ramp shall not be steeper than one unit vertical in 48 units horizontal (2-percent slope).
1012.4	**Vertical rise**: The rise for any ramp run shall be 30 inches maximum.
1012.6.1	**Width:** The clear width of a ramp between handrails, if provided, shall be 36 inches minimum.
1012.6	**Landings**: Ramps shall have landings at the bottom and top of each ramp, points of turning, entrance, exists at doors.
1012.6.1	**Slope:** Landings shall have a slope not steeper than one unit vertical in 48 units horizontal in any direction.
1012.6.2	**Width:** The landing shall be at least as wide as the widest ramp run adjoining the landing.
1012.6.3	**Length**: The landing length shall be 60 inches minimum.
1012.6.4	**Change in direction:** Where changes in the direction of travel occur at landings provided between ramp runs, the landing shall be 60 inches by 60 inches minimum.
1012.8	**Handrails:** Ramps with a rise greater than 6 inches shall have handrails on both sides.
1014	**Handrails**
1014.2	**Height:** Handrail height, measured above stair tread nosings, or finish surface of ramp slop, shall be uniform, not less than 34 inches and not more than 38 inches.
1014.3	**Handrail Graspability**: Required handrails shall comply with Section 1014.3.1 or shall provide equivalent graspability.
1014.3.1	**Type I:** Handrails with a circular cross section shall have an outside diameter of at least 1 ¼ inches and not greater than 2 inches. Where a handrail is not circular, it shall have a perimeter dimension of at least 4 inches and not greater than 6 1/4 inches with a maximum cross section dimension of 2 1/4 inches. Edges shall have a minimum radius of 0.01 inch.
1014.3.2	**Type II:** Handrails with a perimeter greater than 6 1/4 inches provide a graspable finger recess area on both sides of the profile.
1014.7	**Clearance:** Clear space between a handrail and a wall or other surface shall be a minimum of 1 1/2 inches.
1015	**Guards**
1015.2	**Where required:** Guards shall be located along open-sided walking surfaces, including mezzanines, equipment platforms, stairs, ramps and landings that are located more than 30 inches measured vertically to the floor or grade below at any point within 36 inches horizontally to the edge of the open side.

Section #	Highlight
1015.3	**Height:** Required guards shall be not less than 42 inches high, measured vertically as follows: 1. From the adjacent walking surfaces 2. On stairs, from the line connecting the leading edges of the tread nosing. 3. On ramps, from the ramp surface at the guard.
1015.4	**Opening limitations:** Required guards shall not have openings which allow passage of a sphere 4 inches in diameter from the walking surface to the required guard height.
1016	**Exit Access**
1018	**Aisles**
1020	**Corridors**
1028	**Exit Discharge**
1028.1	**General:** Exits shall discharge directly to the exterior of the building. The exit discharge shall be at grade or provide direct access to grade, and it shall not reenter the building.
1029	**Assembly**
1029.7	**Travel distance:** Exits and aisles shall be located so that the travel distance to an exit door shall not be greater than 200 feet measured along the line of travel in non-sprinklered buildings. Travel distance shall not be more than 250 feet in sprinklered buildings.
1029.3	**Common path of egress travel:** The common path of egress travel shall not exceed 30 feet from any seat to a point where an occupant has a choice of two paths of egress travel to two exits.
1030	**Emergency Escape and Rescue**
1030.2	**Minimum size:** Emergency escape and rescue shall have a minimum net clear opening of 5.7 square feet **Exception:** The minimum net clear opening for grade floor emergency escape and rescue openings shall be 5 square feet.
1030.2.1	**Minimum dimensions:** The minimum net clear opening height dimension shall be 24 inches. The minimum net clear width dimension shall be 20 inches.
1030.3	**Maximum height from floor:** Emergency escape and rescue openings shall have a bottom clear opening not greater than 44 inches measured from the floor.
1203	**Ventilation**
1203.2.1	**Openings into attic:** Exterior openings into the attic space of any building intended for human occupancy shall be protected to prevent the entry of birds, squirrels, rodents, snakes and other similar creatures.

Section #	Highlight
1203.4	**Under-floor ventilation**
1203.4. 1	**Openings for under-floor ventilation**: The net area of ventilation openings shall not be less than 1 square foot for each 150 square feet of crawl-space area.
1203.5	**Natural ventilation**
1203.5.1.1	**Adjoining spaces:** Where rooms and spaces without openings to the outdoors are ventilated through an adjoining room, the opening to the adjoining room shall be unobstructed and shall have an area of not less than 8 percent of the floor area of the interior room or space, but not less than 25 square feet.
1205	**Lighting**
1205.2	**Natural light:** The minimum net glazed area shall not be less than 8 percent of the floor area of the room served.
1205.4	**Stairway illumination:** Stairways within dwelling units and exterior stairways serving a dwelling unit shall have an illumination level on tread runs of not less than 1 footcandle.
1208	**Interior Space Dimensions**
1208.1	**Minimum room widths:** Habitable spaces, other than a kitchen, shall not be less than 7 feet in any plan dimension. Kitchens will have a clear passageway of not less than 3 feet.
1208.2	**Minimum ceiling heights**: Occupiable spaces, habitable spaces, and corridors shall have a ceiling height 7 feet 6 inches. Bathrooms, toilet rooms, kitchens … ceiling height not less than 7 feet.
1208.3	**Room area:** Every dwelling unit shall have no fewer one room that shall have not less than 120 square feet of net floor area. Other habitable rooms shall have a net floor area of not less than 70 square feet.
1209	**Access to Unoccupied Spaces**
1209.1	**Crawl Spaces:** Crawl spaces shall be provided with no fewer than one access opening which shall be not less than 18 inches by 24 inches.
1209.2	**Attic spaces:** An opening not less than 20 inches by 30 inches shall be provided to any attic having a clear height area of over 30 inches. Clear headroom of not less than 30 inches shall be provided in the attic space at or above the access opening.
	Chapter 13 — Energy Efficiency - Removed from the FBC-Building volume, it is now a standalone book which is titled: Energy Conservation.
1405	**Installation of Wall Coverings**

Section #	Highlight
1405.7	**Stone veneer:** Stone veneer units not exceeding 10 inches in thickness shall be anchored directly to masonry, concrete or to stud construction by one of the following methods: 1. With concrete or masonry backing 2. With wood stud backing 3. With cold-formed steel stud backing
1405.8	**Slab-type Veneer**
1405.9	**Terra cotta**
1405.10	**Adhered masonry veneer**
1405.11	**Metal veneers**
1405.12	**Glass veneer**
1503	**Weather Protection**
1503.2	**Flashing:** shall be installed in such a manner so as to prevent moisture entering the wall and roof through joints in copings, through moisture-permeable materials and at intersections with parapet walls and other penetrations through the roof plane.
1503.2.1	**Locations:** Flashing shall be installed at wall and roof intersections, at gutters ... with a thickness of not less than provided in Table 1503.2 or in compliance with RAS 111. **Exception:** This requirement does not apply to hip and ridge junctions.
Table 1503.2	**Metal Flashing Material**
1503.3	**Coping:** Parapet walls shall be properly coped with non-combustible, weatherproof materials of a width no less than the thickness of the parapet wall.
1503.4	**Roof drainage:** Unless roofs are sloped to drain over roof edges, design and installation of roof drainage systems shall comply with Section 1503 and the Florida Building Code Plumbing, Chapter 11.
1503.4.3	**Gutters:** Gutters and leaders placed on the outside of buildings, other than Group R-3, private garages and buildings of Type V construction, shall be of non-combustible material or a minimum of Schedule 40 plastic pipe.
1503.7	**Protection against decay and termites**: Condensate lines and roof downspouts shall discharge at least 1 foot away from the structure sidewall .... Gutters with downspouts are required on all buildings with eaves of less than 6 inches horizontal projection except for gable end rakes or on a roof above another roof.
1504	**Performance Requirements**
1504.1	**Wind resistance of roofs**: Roof decks and roof coverings shall be designed for wind loads in accordance with Chapter 16 and Sections 1504.2, 1504.3 and 1504.4

Section #	Highlight
1504.1.1	**Wind resistance of asphalt shingles:** Asphalt shingles shall be designed according to Section 1507.2.7.
1504.2	**Wind resistance of clay and concrete tiles:** Wind loads and clay and concrete tile roof coverings shall be in accordance with Section 1609.5
1504.3	**Wind resistance of non-ballasted roofs:** Roof covering installed on roofs in accordance with Section 1507 that are mechanically attached or adhered to the roof deck shall be designed to resist the design wind load pressures for components and cladding in accordance with Section 1609.
1504.6	**Physical properties:** Roof coverings installed on low-slope roofs (roof slope < 2:12) in accordance with Section 1507 shall demonstrate physical integrity over the working life of the roof based upon 2000 hours of exposure to accelerated weathering tests conducted in accordance with ASTM G152, G153, G154, G155.
1505	**Fire Classification**
1505.2	**Class A roof assemblies:** Class A roof assemblies are those that are effective against severe fire test exposure.
1505.3	**Class B roof assemblies:** Class B roof assemblies are those that are effective against moderate fire- test exposure.
1505.4	**Class C roof assemblies:** Class C roof assemblies are those that are effective against light fire-test exposure.
1505.6	**Fire retardant-treated wood and shingles and shakes:** Fire retardant-treated wood shakes and shingles shall be treated by impregnation with chemicals by the full-cell vacuum-pressure process, in accordance with AWPA C1.
1506	**Materials**
1506.2	**Compatibility of materials:** Roofs and roof coverings shall be of materials that are compatible with each other and with the building or structure to which the materials are applied.
1506.4	**Product Identification:** Roof-covering materials shall be delivered in packages bearing the manufacturer's identifying marks and approved testing agency labels required in accordance with Section 1505.
1507	**Requirements for Roof Coverings**
1507.2	**Asphalt shingles**
1507.2.1	**Deck requirements:** Asphalt shingles shall be fastened to solidly sheathed decks.

Section #	Highlight
1507.2.2	**Slope:** Asphalt shingles shall only be used on roof slopes of two units vertical in 12 units horizontal or greater. For roof slopes from two units vertical in 12 units horizontal up to four units vertical in 12 units horizontal with slopes between 2:12 and 4:12 double underlayment application is required.
1507.2.6	**Fasteners:** Fasteners for asphalt shingles shall be galvanized, stainless steel ... minimum 12 gage shank with a 3/8-inch diameter head, of a length to penetrate through the roofing materials and a minimum of ¾ inch into the roof sheathing.
1507.2.7	**Attachment:** Asphalt shingles shall be secured to roof with not less than four fasteners per strip shingle or two 2 fasteners per individual shingle.
1507.2.9.1	**Base and Counter Flashings:** Base and counter flashing shall be installed as follows: 3. A continuous metal minimum 4 inch X 4 inch "L" flashing... shall be fastened 6 inches on center with approved fasteners. All laps shall be a minimum of 4 inches fully sealed in approved flashing cement.
1507.2.9.2	**Valleys:** Valley linings shall be installed in accordance with the manufacturer's instructions before applying shingles. Valley linings of the following types shall be permitted: 1. For open valleys (valley lining exposed) lined with metal 2. For open valleys, valley lining of two piles of mineral-surfaced roll roofing 3. For closed valleys (valleys covered with shingles)
1507.2.9.3	**Drip edge:** Provide drip edge at eaves and gables of shingle roofs. Overlap to be a minimum of 3 inches. Eave drip edges shall extend 1/2 inch below sheathing and extend back on the roof a minimum of 2 inches ... Drip edge shall be mechanically fastened a maximum of 12 inches o.c....the mean roof height exceeds 33 feet drip edges shall be mechanically fastened a maximum of 4 inches on center.
1507.3	**Clay and concrete tile:** The installation of clay and concrete tile shall comply with the provisions of this section.
1507.3.3	**Underlayment:** Unless otherwise noted, required underlayment shall conform to ASTM D 226, Type II, ASTM D 1970; ASTM D 2626 or ASTM D 6380.
1507.3.4	**Clay tile:** Clay roof tile shall comply with ASTM C 1167.
1507.3.5	**Concrete tile:** Concrete roof tile shall comply with ASTM C 1492.
1507.3.6	**Fasteners:** Tile fasteners shall be corrosion resistant not less than 11 gage, 5/16 inch head, and of sufficient length to penetrate the deck a minimum of 0.75 inches or through he thickness of the deck, whichever is is less.
1507.3.7	**Attachment:** Clay and concrete roof tiles shall be fastened in accordance with Section 1609 or with FRSA/TRI Florida High Wind Concrete and clay Roof Tile Installation Manual.
1507.3.8	**Application:** Tile shall be applied according to the manufacturer's installation instructions ... or the recommendation of RAS 118, 119 or 120.

Section #	Highlight
1507.4	**Metal roof panels:** The installation of metal roof panels shall comply with the provisions of this section.
1507.4.2	**Deck slope:** Minimum slopes for metal roof panels shall comply with the following: 1. The minimum slope for lapped, nonsoldered seam metal roofs without applied lap sealant 2. The minimum slope for lapped, non-soldered seam metal roofs with applied lap sealant 3. The minimum slope for standing seam roof systems
1507.4.3	**Material Standards:** Metal-sheet roof covering systems that incorporate structural members … shall be installed over structural decking shall comply with Table 1507.4.3(1).
Table 1507.4.3(2)	**Minimum Corrosion Resistance**
1507.5	**Metal roof shingles**
1507.5.2	**Deck slope:** Metal roof shingles shall not be installed on roof slopes below three units vertical in 12 units horizontal (25-percent slope).
1507.5.7	**Flashing**: Roof valley flashing shall be of corrosion-resistant metal of the same material as the roof covering …The valley flashing shall extend at least 8 inches from the centerline each way and shall have a splash diverter rib not less than 0.75 inch at the flow line formed as part of the flashing. Sections of flashing shall have an end lap of not less than 4 inches.
1507.6	**Mineral-surfaced roll roofing**
1507.6.2	**Deck slope**: Mineral –surfaced roll roofing shall not be applied on roof slopes below one unit vertical in 12 units horizontal. .
1507.7	**Slate shingles:** The installation of slate shingles shall comply with the provisions of this section.
1507.7.6	**Application:** Minimum headlap for slate shingles shall be installed in accordance with table 1507.7.6 and be secured to the roof with two fasteners per slate.
Table 1507.7.6	**Slate Shingle Headlap**
1507.7.7	**Flashing:** Flashing and counterflashing shall be made with sheet metal. Valley flashing shall be a minimum of 16 inches wide. Valley and flashing metal shall be a minimum thickness, provided in Table 1503.2.
1507.8	**Wood shingles**
Table 1507.8.5	**Wood Shingles Material Requirements**

Section #	Highlight
1507.9	**Wood shakes:** The installation of wood shakes shall be limited to roofs where allowable uplift resistance is equal to or greater than the design uplift pressure for the roof in compliance with Section 1504.1.
Table 1507.9.6	**Wood Shake Material Requirements.**
1507.10	**Built-up roofs:** The installation of built-up roofs shall comply with the provisions of this section.
1507.10.1	**Slope:** Built-up roofs shall have a design slope of a minimum one-fourth unit vertical in 12 units horizontal for drainage, except for coal-tar built-up roofs that shall have a design slope of a minimum one-eighth unit vertical in 12 units horizontal.
Table 1507.10.2	**Built-Up Roofing Material Standards**
1507.11	**Modified bitumen roofing:** The installation of modified bitumen roofing shall comply with the provisions of this section.
1507.11.1	**Slope:** Modified bitumen membrane roofs shall have a design slope of a minimum of one-fourth unit vertical in 12 units horizontal (2-percent slope) for drainage.
1507.12	**Thermoset single-ply roofs:** The installation of thermoset single-ply roofing shall comply with the provisions of this section.
1507.12.1	**Slope:** Thermoset single-ply membrane roofs shall have a design slope of a minimum of one-fourth unit vertical in 12 units horizontal (2-percent slope).
1507.12.2	**Material standards**: Thermoset single-ply membrane roof coverings shall comply with ASTM D 4637, ASTM D 5019, or CGSB 37-GP-52M.
1507.13	**Thermoplastic single-ply roofs:** The installation of thermoplastic single-ply roofing shall comply with the provisions of this section.
1507.13.1	**Slope:** Thermoplastic single-ply membrane roofs shall have a design slope of a minimum of one-fourth unit vertical in 12 units horizontal (2-percent slope).
1507.14	**Sprayed polyurethane foam:** The installation of spray polyurethane foam shall comply with the provisions of this section or in compliance with RAS 109 and 109-A.
1507.14.1	**Slope:** Sprayed polyurethane foam shall have a design slope of a minimum of one-fourth unit vertical in 12 units horizontal (2-percent slope) for drainage.
1507.14.3	**Application:** A liquid applied protective coating that complies with Table 1507.14.3 shall be applied no less than 2 hours nor more than 72 hours following the application of the foam.
1507.15	**Liquid-applied roofing:** The installation of liquid-applied roofing shall comply with the provisions of this section.

Section #	Highlight
1507.15.1	**Slope:** Liquid-applied roofing shall have a design slope of a minimum of one-fourth unit vertical in 12 units horizontal (2-percent slope).
1510	**Rooftop Structures**
1509.2	**Penthouses:** Penthouses in compliance with Sections 1510.2.1 through 1510.2.5 shall be considered as a portion of the story directly below the roof deck on which such penthouses are located.
1510.2.1	**Height above roof deck**: Penthouses constructed on buildings of other than Type I construction shall not exceed 18 feet in height above the roof deck as measured to the average height of the roof of the penthouse.
Table 1510.10	**Clearance Below Raised Roof Mounted Mechanical Units**
1511	**Existing Roofing**
1511.1	**General: Exception:** Reroofing shall not be required to meet the minimum design slope requirement ... for roofs that provide positive roof drainage.
1511.3	**Recovering vs. replacement**: New roof coverings shall not be installed without first removing all existing layers of roof coverings down to the roof deck where any of the following conditions occur: Highlight 1 -5.
1512	**High-Velocity Hurricane Zones - General**
1513	**High-Velocity Hurricane Zones - Definitions:** - Architectural metal panel - Discontinuous roofing system - RAS
1514	**High-Velocity Hurricane Zones - Weather Protection**
1514.2	**Flashings**
1514.2.1	**Locations**: Where flashing is of metal, the metal shall conform with the provisions of RAS 111.
1514.2.4.1	Metal counterflashing shall be built into walls, set in reglets or applied as stucco type and shall be turned down over base flashing not less than 3 inches.
1514.2.4.2	Metal counterflashing shall be side lapped a minimum of 4 inches.
1514.2.5	**Roof penetration flashing**
1514.2.5.1	All pipes shall be flashed with approved lead sleeve-type, pitch pans ... Lead flashing shall not be less than 2.5 pounds per square foot. Flanges shall be a minimum of 4 inches.

Section #	Highlight
1514.4.2	**Overflow drains and scuppers:** .Where roof drains are required, overflow drains or overflow scupper sized in accordance with Florida Building Code, Plumbing shall be installed with the inlet flow line located not less than 2 inches or more than 4 inches above the low point of the finished roofing surface, excluding sumps. Overflow scuppers shall be a minimum of 4 inches in any dimension and shall be located as close as practical to required vertical leaders, conductors or downspouts.
1515	**High-Velocity Hurricane Zones - Performance Requirement**
1515.1.5	No loose laid ballasted or non-ballasted system shall be allowed.
1515.2	**Guidelines for roofing applications**
Table 1515.2	**Minimum slope**
1515.2.2.1	In new construction, the minimum deck slope shall not be less than ¼:12.
1517	**High-Velocity Hurricane Zones - Materials**
1517.5	**Fasteners**
1517.5.1	Nails shall be minimum 12 gage, annular ring shank nails having not less than 20 rings per inch, heads not less than 3/8 inch in diameter; and lengths sufficient to penetrate through the thickness of plywood panel or wood plank not less than 3/16 inch, or to penetrate into a 1 inch or greater thickness of lumber not less than 1 inch.
1517.5.2	Such fasteners shall be applied through "tin caps" no less than 1 5/8 and not more than 2 inches in diameter and of not less than 32 gage sheet metal. "Cap nails" ... complying with this section shall be an acceptable substitute.
1517.6	**Metal roofing accessories:** All metal accessories for roofs shall not less than 26 gage G-90 galvanized or stainless steel, 16 oz. copper, 0.025 inch thick aluminum, lead sheet with a minimum 2.5 pounds per square foot or equivalent.
1517.6.2	Gravel stop or drip edge profiles shall be as follows: Highlight from Sections 1517.6.2.1, 1517.6.2.2, 1517.6.2.4, 1517.6.2.5, 1517.6.2.6.
1518	**High-Velocity Hurricane Zones – Roof Coverings with Slopes 2:12 or Greater**
1518.5	**Fiber cement shingles:** Fiber-cement shingles shall be applied in compliance with ... shall meet the following minimum requirements.
1518.5.1	All non-asbestos fiber-cement shingles shall conform to ASTM C 1225.
1518.7	**Asphaltic shingles:** Asphaltic shingles layout, alignment and placement of mechanical attachment ... shall be installed in accordance with RAS 115.
1518.7.2	Installation of all asphaltic shingles shall be limited to a roof mean height of 33 feet, unless otherwise specifically noted in the product approval.

Section #	Highlight
1518.7.3.2	Asphaltic shingles shall be installed in compliance with the product approval, but in no case with less than six approved roofing nails or approved fastening devices which penetrate the sheathing a minimum of 3/16 inch or penetrate into a 1 inch or greater thickness of lumber a minimum of 1 inch.
1518.8.4	**All tiles systems**
1518.8.4.1	Roof tile systems, combining mechanically fastened tile and mortar and/or adhesive, shall be acceptable.
1518.8.4.2	In an air permeable tile roofing systems, (1) length of tile not less than 12 inches and not greater than 21 inches and the exposed width shall be between 8.5 inches and 15 inches; (2) the maximum thickness of the nose of the tile shall not exceed 1.3 inches; (3) mortar or adhesive set system shall have at least two-thirds of the tile free of mortar and/or adhesive contact.
1518.8.7	Tile systems shall extend beyond the drip edge (not including the rake) not less than 3/4 inch but not more than 2 inches.
1518.8.10	Mortar or adhesive set tiles applied at an incline from 6:12 up to and including 7:12 shall have the first course of tile (this applies to pan only on two-piece barrel tile) mechanically fastened with not less than one fastener per tile.
1518.10	**Wood shingles and shakes:** Installation of all wood shingles and shakes shall be limited to a roof mean height of 33 feet, unless otherwise specifically noted in the product approval.
1519	**High-Velocity Hurricane Zones – Roof Coverings with Slopes Less than 2:12**
1520	**High-Velocity Hurricane Zones – Insulation**
1520.5	**Application:** Roof insulation shall be applied in strict compliance with the application methods ... set forth in RAS 117.
1520.5.1	Roof insulation, either on the ground or on the roof top shall be kept dry. The building official shall instruct the removal of insulation … where panels cannot achieve 85-percent adhesion.
1520.5.2	When applied in hot asphalt or cold adhesive, no insulation panel's dimension shall be greater than 4 feet.
1520.5.3	Strip or spot mopping of insulation panels shall be used as an application method only when approved in the product approval.
1521	**High-Velocity Hurricane Zones – Reroofing**
1521.4	Not more than 25 percent of the total roof area or roof section of any existing building or structure shall be repaired, replaced or recovered in any 12-month period unless the entire existing roofing system or roof section is replaced to conform to requirements of this code.

Section #	Highlight
1521.16	No recover application shall take place over existing wood shingles, shakes, slate, tile or metal shingles.
1522	**High-Velocity Hurricane Zones – Rooftop Structures and Components**
Table 1522.3	**Roof Mounted Equipment Height Requirements**
1523	**High-Velocity Hurricane Zones – Testing**
1523.6.5.2.6	**Fiber cement shingle or tile panels**: All fiber-cement shingles or tiles shall resist a minimum wind uplift resistance as determined by Chapter 16 (HVHZ) for a roof slope of 9.5 degrees and a roof mean height of 15 feet.
1524	**High-Velocity Hurricane Zones – Required Owners Notification for Roofing Considerations**
1524.1	**Scope:** As it pertains to this section, it is the responsibility of the roofing contractor to provide the owner with the required roofing permit. .
1603	**Construction Documents**
1603.1	**General:** Construction documents shall show the size, section, and relative locations of structural members … required by section 1603.1.1 through 1603.1.8 shall be indicated on the construction documents.
1607	**Live Loads**
Table 1607.1	**Minimum Uniformly Distributed Live Loads and Minimum Concentrated Live Loads**
1607.8.1	**Handrails and Guards**: Handrails and guards shall be designed to resist a linear load of 50 pounds per linear foot in accordance with section 4.5.1 of ASCE 7.
1607.12	**Roof Loads**
1609	**Wind Loads**
1609.1.2	**Protection of openings: Exceptions:** 1. Wood structural panels with a minimum thickness of 7/16 inch and maximum panel span of 8 feet shall be permitted for opening protection in one- and two-story buildings classified as Group R-3 or R-4 occupancy.
Figure 1609.3(1)	**Ultimate design wind speeds for Risk Category II buildings and other structures.**
Figure 1609.3(2)	**Ultimate design wind speeds for Risk Category III and IV buildings and other structures.**
Figure 1609.3	**Ultimate design wind speeds for Risk Category I buildings and other structures.**
1615	**Structural Integrity**

Section #	Highlight
1709	**Preconstruction Load Tests**
1709.5	**Exterior window and door assemblies**
1709.5.1	**Exterior window and doors:** Exterior windows and sliding doors shall be tested and labeled as conforming to AAMA/WDMA/CSA101/I.S.2/A440 or TAS 202 (HVHZ shall comply with TAS 202 and ASTM E1300 or Section 2404).
1803	**Geotechnical Investigations**
1803.1	**General:** Where required by the building official or where geotechnical investigations involve in-situ testing, laboratory testing or engineering calculations, such investigations shall be conducted by a registered design professional.
1803.2	**Investigation required:** Geotechnical investigations shall be conducted in accordance with Sections 1803.3 - 1803.5.
	Exception: The building official shall be permitted to waive the requirement for a geotechnical investigation .... Conditions in Sections 1803.5.1 through 1803.5.6 and Sections 1803.5.10 and 1803.5.11.
1803.5	**Investigated conditions:** Geotechnical investigations shall be conducted as indicated in Sections 1803.5.1 – 1803.5.12.
1803.5.2	**Questionable soil:** Where the classification, strength or compressibility of the soil is in doubt ... the building official shall be permitted to require that a geotechnical investigation be conducted.
1803.5.4	**Ground-water table:** A subsurface soil investigation shall be performed to determine whether the existing ground-water table is above or within 5 feet below the elevation of the lowest floor.
	Exception: A subsurface soil investigation ... shall not be required where waterproofing is provided in accordance with Section 1805.
1803.6	**Reporting:** This geotechnical report shall include, but need not to be limited to the following information: Highlight 1 -10.
1804	**Excavation, Grading, and Fill**
1804.3	**Placement of backfill:** The excavation outside the foundation shall be backfilled with soil ... or with controlled low-strength material (CLSM).
1804.6	**Compacted fill material:** Where shallow foundations will bear on compacted fill material, the compacted fill shall comply with the provisions of an approved geotechnical report, as set forth in Section 1803.
1805	**Dampproofing and Waterproofing**

Section #	Highlight
1805.1	**General:** Walls or portions thereof that retain earth and enclose interior spaces and floors below grade shall be waterproofed and damp proofed in accordance with this section.
1805.3.2	**Walls: Walls** required to be waterproofed shall be of concrete or masonry and shall be designed and constructed to withstand the hydrostatic pressures and other lateral loads to which the walls will be subjected. Waterproofing shall be applied from the bottom of the wall to not less than 12 inches above the maximum elevation of the ground-water table.
1805.4.2	**Foundation drain:** The drain shall extend a minimum of 12 inches beyond the outside edge of the footing. The pipe or tile shall be placed on not less than 2 inches of gravel or crushed stone complying with section 1805.4.1 and shall be covered with not less than 6 inches of the same material.
1806	**Presumptive Load-Bearing Values of Soils**
Table 1806.2	**Presumptive Load-Bearing Values**
1807	**Foundation Walls, Retaining Walls and Embedded Posts and Poles**
1807.1.6.1	**Foundation wall thickness**: The thickness of prescriptively designed foundation walls shall not be less than the thickness of the wall supported, except that foundation walls of at least 8-inch nominal width shall be permitted to support brick veneered frame walls and 10 inch wide cavity walls provided the requirements of Section 1807.1.6.2 or 1807.1.6.3 are met.
Table 1807.1.6.3(1)	**Plain Masonry Foundation Walls**
1808	**Foundations**
1808.7.4	**Foundation elevation:** On graded sites, top of any exterior foundation shall extend above the elevation of the street gutter at point of discharge of the inlet of an approved drainage device a minimum of 12 inches plus 2 percent.
1809	**Shallow Foundations**
1809.2	**Supporting soils:** Shallow foundations shall be built on undisturbed soil, compacted fill material or controlled low-strength material (CLSM).
Table 1809.7	**Prescriptive Footings Supporting Walls of Light-Frame Construction**
1810	**Deep Foundations**
1810.3.5.2.1	**Cased:** Cast-in-place deep foundation elements with a permanent casing shall have a nominal outside diameter of not less than 8 inches.

Section #	Highlight
1810.3.5.2.2	**Uncased:** Cast-in-place deep foundation elements without a permanent casing shall have a diameter of not less than 12 inches. The element length shall not exceed 30 times the average diameter.
1810.3.8	**Precast concrete piles:** Precast concrete piles shall be designed and detailed in accordance with Sections 1810.3.8.1 – 1810.3.8.3.
1810.3.8.2.1	**Minimum reinforcement:** Longitudinal reinforcement shall consist of at least four bars with a minimum longitudinal reinforcement ratio of 0.008.
1901.5	**Construction documents:** The construction documents for structural concrete construction shall include: Highlight 1 – 11.
1903	**Specifications for Tests and Materials**
1903.1	**General:** Materials used to produce concrete … shall comply with the applicable standards listed in ACI 318.
1904	**Durability Requirements**
1904.1	**Structural concrete:** Structural concrete shall conform to the durability requirements of ACI 318.
1907	**Minimum Slab Provisions**
1907.1	**General**: The thickness of concrete floor slabs supported directly on the ground shall not be less than 3 1/2 inches. A 6-mil polyethylene vapor retarder with joints lapped not less than 6 inches shall be placed between the base course … shall be used to retard vapor transmission through the floor slab. **Exception:** A vapor retarded is not required: 1. For detached structures 2. For unheated storage rooms 3. For buildings and other occupancies 4. For driveways, walks, patios 5. Where approved based on local site conditions
2002	**Materials**
2002.3	**Screen enclosures**
2002.3.1	**Thickness:** Actual wall thickness of extruded aluminum members shall not be less not less than 0.040 inch.
2002.3.3	**Vinyl, tempered glass, and acrylic panels.** Vinyl and acrylic panels shall be removable. Removable panels shall be identified as removable by a decal.
2003.7.5.1	All expansion anchors shall not be installed less than 3 inches from the edge of the concrete slab and/or footings.

Section #	Highlight
2003.8.2	**Structural aluminum decking and siding**
2003.8.2.3	Aluminum sheets shall be secured to the supports to adequately resist positive and negative loads. Attachments shall be at intervals not exceeding 8 inches o.c. and shall be secured to each other at side laps at intervals as required by rational analysis, but shall not exceed 12 inches o.c.
2111	**Masonry Fireplaces**
2111.1	**General:** The construction of masonry fireplaces, consisting of concrete or masonry, shall be in accordance with this section.
2111.8.1	**Damper:** Masonry fireplaces shall be equipped with a ferrous metal damper located at least 8 inches above top of fireplace opening. Dampers shall be installed in the fireplace …and shall be operable from the room containing the fireplace.
2111.9.1	**Hearth thickness:** The minimum thickness of fireplace hearths shall be 4 inches.
2111.11	**Hearth extension dimensions:** .Hearth extension shall extend not less than 16 inches in front of, and at least 8 inches beyond, each side of the fireplace opening. Where the fireplace opening is 6 square feet or larger, the extension shall extend at least 20 inches in front and 12 inches beyond each side of the opening.
Figure 2111.11	**Illustration of Exception to Fireplace Clearance Provision**
2112	**Masonry Heaters**
2112.3	**Footings and Foundations:** The firebox floor shall be a minimum thickness of 4 inches of noncombustible material and be supported on a noncombustible footing.
2112.5	**Masonry heater clearance:** Combustible materials shall not be placed within 36 inches of the outside surface of a masonry heater in accordance with NFPA 211.
	Exception: 1.When the masonry heater wall thickness 8 inches thick of solid masonry and the wall thickness of the heat exchange channels is at least 5 inches thick of solid masonry, combustible materials shall not be placed within 4 inches of the outside surface of a masonry heater.
2113	**Masonry Chimneys**
2113.5	**Corbeling:** Masonry chimneys shall not be corbelled more than half of the chimney's wall thickness from a wall or foundation, nor shall it be corbelled from a wall or foundation that is less than 12 inches in thickness unless it projects equally on each side of the wall.
2113.19	**Chimney Clearances:** Any portion of masonry chimney located in the interior of the building or within the exterior wall of the building shall have a minimum airspace clearance to combustibles of 2 inches.
2119	**High-Velocity Hurricane Zones – Quality, Tests, and Approvals**

Section #	Highlight
2203	**Identification and Protection of Steel for Structural Purposes**
2203.1	**Identification:** Identification of structural steel members shall comply with the requirements contained in AISC 360.
2221	**High-Velocity Hurricane Zones – General - Open Web Steel Joists**
2221.6	**End supports and anchorage**
2221.6.1	Joists not bear directly on unit masonry unless masonry is designed as engineered unit masonry with properly reinforced, grout-filled continuous bond beam.
2224	**High-Velocity Hurricane Zones - Chain Link Fence**
2224.2	Chain link fences less than 12 feet in height shall be designed according to the loads specified in Chapter 16 (HVHZ) or as in Table 2224.
Table 2224	**Chain Link Fence Minimum Requirements**
2303	**Minimum Standards and Quality**
2303.1.1	**Sawn lumber:** Sawn lumber used for load supporting purposes... shall be identified by the grade mark of a lumber grading or inspection agency that has been approved by an accreditation body that complies with DOC PS 20 or equivalent.
2303.1.6	**Fiberboard:** Fiberboard for its various uses shall conform to ASTM C 208.
2303.1.5.2	**Roof insulation**: Where used as roof insulation in all types of construction, fiberboard shall be protected with an approved roof covering.
2303.1.6.3.1	**Protection:** Fiberboard wall insulation applied on the exterior of foundation walls shall be protected below ground level with a bituminous coating.
2303.1.8	**Particleboard:** Particleboard shall conform to ANSI A208.1.
2303.1.8.1	**Floor underlayment:** Type PBU underlayment shall not be less than 1/4 -inch and shall be installed in accordance with the instructions of the Composite Panel Association.
2303.1.9.2	**Moisture Content:** Where preservative treated wood is used in enclosed locations.... such wood shall be at a moisture content of 19 percent or less before being covered with insulation, interior wall finish, floor covering or other material.
2303.2	**Fire retardant-treated wood:** Fire-retardant-treated wood is any wood product which... a listed flame spread index of 25 or less and show no evidence of significant progressive combustion when the test is continued for an additional 20-minute period.
2303.2.4	**Labeling:** Fire-retardant-treaded lumber and wood structural panels shall be labeled. The label shall contain the following items: Highlight 1 - 8.

Section #	Highlight
2303.4	**Trusses:** wood trusses shall comply with Sections 2303.4.1 – 2303.4.7.
2303.6	**Nails and staples**: Nails used for framing and sheathing connections shall have a minimum average bending yield strength … shank diameters of at least 0.099 inch but not larger than 0.142 inch.
2304	**General Construction Requirements**
Table 2308.5.11	**Minimum Thickness of Wall Sheathing**
Table 2304.6.1	**Maximum Nominal Design Wind Speed Permitted for Wood Structural panel wall Sheathing Used to Resist Wind Pressures**
2304.8	**Floor and roof sheathing:** Structural floor sheathing and structural roof sheathing shall comply with sections 2304.8.1 and 2304.8.2 respectively.
Table 2304.8(1)	**Allowable Spans for Lumber Floor and Roof Sheathing**
Table 2304.8(2)	**Sheathing Lumber, Minimum Grade Requirements: Board Grade**
2304.9.3	**Mechanically laminated decking:** Mechanically laminated decking consists of square-edged dimension lumber laminations set on edge and nailed to the adjacent pieces and to the supports.
2304.9.3.2	**Nailing:** The length of nails connecting laminations shall not be less than two and one-half times the net thickness of each lamination.
2304.12	**Protection against decay and termites**: Wood shall be protected from decay and termites in accordance with the applicable provisions of Sections 2304.12.1 – 2304.12.7.
2304.12.1.1	**Joists, girders, subfloor:** Where wood joists or the bottom of wood structural floor without joists are closer than 18 inches, or wood girders are closer than 12 inches to the exposed ground … shall be of naturally durable or preservative treated wood.
2304.12.1.2	**Wood supported by exterior foundation:** Wood framing members, including wood sheathing that rest on exterior foundation walls and are less than 8 inches from exposed earth shall be of naturally durable or preservative- treated wood.
2304.12.1.4	**Sleepers and sills:** Sleepers and sills on a concrete or masonry slab that is in direct contact with earth shall be of naturally durable or preservative treated wood.
2304.12.1.5	**Wood siding:** Clearance between wood siding and earth on the exterior of a building shall not be less than 6 inches or less than 2 inches vertical from concrete steps … exposed to the weather except where siding, sheathing and wall framing are of naturally durable or preservative- treated wood.
2304.12.2.2	**Posts and columns:** Posts and columns supporting permanent structures and supported by concrete or masonry slab or footing that is in direct contact with earth shall be of naturally durable or preservative-treated wood.
	Exceptions: 1 - 2.

Section #	Highlight
2304.12.9	**Preparation of building site and removal of debris**
2304.12.9.2	The foundation and the area encompassed within 1 foot … and the fill material free of vegetation and foreign material.
2304.12.9.3	After all work is completed, loose wood and debris shall be completely removed from under the building and within 1 foot thereof.
2304.13	**Long-term loading**: Wood members supporting concrete, masonry or similar materials …shall be limited in accordance with Section 1604.3.1 for these supported materials.
2305	**General Design Requirements for Lateral-Force Resisting Systems**
2305.1	**General:** Structures using wood-frame shear walls... shall be designed and constructed in accordance with AWC SDPWS and the provisions of Sections 2305, 2306 and 2307.
2308	**Conventional Light-Frame Construction**
2308.1	**General:** Detached one- and two- family dwellings and multiple family dwellings (townhouses) not more than 3 stories above grade plane in height with a separate means of egress and their accessory structures shall comply with the Florida Building Code, Residential.
2308.1.2	**Connections and fasteners:** Connections and fasteners used in conventional construction shall comply with the requirements of Section 2304.10.
2308.3.1	**Foundations plates and sills:** Bolts shall be embedded at least 7 inches into concrete or masonry, and spaced not more than 6 feet apart.
2308.4.3.2	**Framing details:** Joist framing from opposite sides of a beam, girder or partition shall be lapped at least 3 inches or the opposing joists shall be tied together in an approved manner.
2308.4.4	**Framing Around Openings**: Trimmer and header joists shall be doubled, or of a lumber of equivalent cross section, where the span of the header exceeds 4 feet.
Table 2308.4.2.1(1)	**Floor joist spans for common lumber species**
Table 2308.4.2.1(2)	**Floor joist spans for common lumber species**
Table 2308.5.1	**Size, height and spacing of wood studs**
2308.5.3.2	**Top plates:** Bearing and exterior wall studs shall be capped with double top plates installed to provide overlapping at corners and at intersections with other partitions. End joints in double top plates should be offset at least 48 inches.
2308.7	**Roof and ceiling framing:** The framing details required in this section apply to roofs having a minimum slope of … valleys shall be designed as beams.
Table 2308.7.1(1)	**Ceiling joists spans for common lumber species**

Section #	Highlight
Table 2308.7.1(1)	**Ceiling joists spans for common lumber species**
Table 2308.7.2(1)	**Rafter spans for common lumber species**
Table 2308.7.2(2)	**Rafter spans for common lumber species**
2308.7.4	**Notches and holes**: Notching at the ends of rafters shall not exceed one fourth the depth. Notches in the top or bottom of the rafter or ceiling joist shall not exceed one sixth the depth and shall not be located in the middle one third of the span, except that a notch not exceeding one third of the depth is permitted in the top of the rafter or ceiling joist not further from the face of the support than the depth of the member. Holes bored in rafters or ceiling joists shall not be within 2 inches of the top and bottom and their diameter shall not exceed 1/3 the depth of the member.
2317	**High-Velocity Hurricane Zones – Unit Stresses**
2317.1.1	Lumber used for joists, rafters, trusses, columns, beams and other structural members shall be no less strength than No. 2 grade Southern Pine, Douglas-Fir Larch, Hem-Fir, or Spruce-Pine –Fir.
2318	**High-Velocity Hurricane Zones - Vertical Framing**
2318.1.2	**Spacing:** Studs shall be spaced not more than 16 inches on center.
2318.1.4	**Sill and/or base plates**
2318.1.4.1	Sills and/or base plates, where provided in contact with masonry …1/2-inch diameter bolts with oversized washer spaced not over 2' feet apart and embedded 7 inches into a grout filled call of masonry or into concrete. Base plates shall be placed in a recess 3/4 inch deep.
2318.1.9	**Notching**
2318.1.9.1	Studs that carry over 75 percent of their capacity shall not be notched or cut.
2318.1.9.2	Studs that carry loads 75 percent or less of their capacity may be notched one-third of the depth without limit of the number of consecutive studs.
2319	**High-Velocity Hurricane Zones - Horizontal Framing**
2319.5	**Notching and boring**
2319.5.1.1	Notches may be cut in the top or bottom not deeper than one-sixth of the depth not longer than one-third of the depth of the member and shall not be located in middle third of span.
2319.7	**Wood entering masonry or reinforced concrete**
2319.7.1	Wood joists, beams, and girders … shall have a minimum of 1/2 inch air space at the top, end and sides or shall be preservative pressure treated or an approved durable species.

Section #	Highlight
2319.12	**Roof Rafters**
2319.17.1	**Trussed rafters**
2319.17.1.2	Where a ceiling is to be attached directly to the underside of trusses, the trusses shall be laterally braced … This lateral bracing shall be restrained at each end and at 20-foot intervals.
2321	**High-Velocity Hurricane Zones - Anchorage**
2321.5	**Anchorage to concrete**
2321.5.1	Anchorage designed to resist uplift forces, securing wood to concrete shall be steel straps embedded in the concrete minimum 4 inches with hooking devices ... set forth by the design professional.
2322	**High-Velocity Hurricane Zones - Sheathing**
2322.1	**Floor sheathing**
2322.1.4	Lumber subflooring shall be not less than 5/8-inch thick when joists … when joists are spaced no more than 24-inches on center.
Table 2322.1.6	**Plywood Subfloor**
2322.1.8	Flooring shall be nailed with 8d common nails up to 3/4", 10d common or 8d ring shank when greater than 3/4 inch thick up to 1 1/8 inches thick.
2322.2	**Roof sheathing**
2322.2.2	Board roof sheathing shall have a net thickness of not less than 3/4 inch when the span is not more than 28 inches or 5/8 when the span is not more than 24 inches with staggered joints and nailed with 8d common nails not less than two in each 6 inch board nor three in each 8 inch board.
2322.2.3	Plywood roof sheathing shall be rated for exposure 1, have a nominal thickness of 19/32 inch and shall be continuous over two or more spans.
Table 2322.2.3	**Allowable Span for Plywood Roof Sheathing**
2322.2.5	Nail spacing shall be 6 inches on center at edges and at intermediate supports. Nail spacing shall be 4 inches on center at gable ends with either 8d ring shank nails or 10d common nails.
Table 2324.1	**Nail Connection for Wood Members**
2326	**High-Velocity Hurricane Zones - Protection of Wood**
2328	**High-Velocity Hurricane Zones - Wood Fences**

Section #	Highlight
2328.2	Fences not exceeding 6 feet in height, shall be constructed to meet the following minimum requirements… embedded 2 feet into a concrete footing 10 inches in diameter and 2-feet deep.
2328.3	Fences not exceeding 5 feet or 4 feet in height shall be constructed as in Section 2328.2 but the spacing of posts may be increased to 5 feet and 6 feet on center for these heights respectively.
2403	**General Requirements for Glass**
2403.1	**Identification:** Each pane shall bear the manufacturer's mark designating the type and thickness of the glass or glazing material.
2405	**Sloped Glazing and Skylights**
2405.1	**Scope:** This section applies to the installation of glass at a slope more than 15 degrees … sloped walls.
2405.3	**Screening:** Where used in monolithic glazing systems, heat strengthened glass and fully tempered glass shall have screens installed below the glazing material.... (1) capable of supporting twice the weight of the glazing (2) be firmly and substantially fastened to the framing members and (3) to be installed within 4 inches of the glass. The screens shall be constructed of a noncombustible material not thinner than No. 12 B&S gage with mesh not larger than 1 x 1 inches. Exceptions — Number 5 for Groups R-2, R-3 and 4 include sections 5.1 and 5.2.
2405.4	**Framing:** Type 1 and 2... frames shall be constructed of noncombustible materials.... Skylights set at an angle of less than 45 degrees... mounted at least 4 inches above the plane of the roof. Skylights shall not be installed in the plane of the roof where the roof pitch is less than 45 degrees from the horizontal.
2412	**High-Velocity Hurricane Zones - Glass Veneer**
2412.3	**Attachment:** Every glass veneer unit shall be attached to backing with approved mastic cement and corrosion-resistant ties.
2412.3.1	Where more than 6 ft above grade, veneer shall be supported by shelf angles, and ties shall be used in both horizontal and vertical joints.
2412.3.2	Veneering shall not be supported on construction which is not an integral part of the wall, and over sidewalks shall be supported on a shelf angle not less than ¼ inch above grade.
2413	**High-Velocity Hurricane Zones - Storm Shutters/External Protective Devices**
2413.1	**General:** Unless exterior wall components including but not limited to structural glazing... all such components shall be protected by product approved storm shutters.
2414	**High-Velocity Hurricane Zones - Curtain Walls**

Section #	Highlight
2504	**Vertical and Horizontal Assemblies**
2504.1.1	**Wood framing:** Wood supports for lath or gypsum board ... shall not less than 2 inches nominal thickness in the least dimension. **Exception:** The minimum nominal dimension of wood furring strips installed over soli backing shall not be less than 1 inch by 2 inches.
2506	**Gypsum Board and Gypsum Panel Materials**
2507	**Lathing and Plastering**
Table 2506.2	**Gypsum Board and Gypsum panel Products Materials and Accessories**
Table 2507.2	**Lath, Plastering Materials and Accessories**
2508	**Gypsum Construction**
Table 2508.1	**Installation of Gypsum Construction**
2508.3	**Single-ply application:** Edges and ends of gypsum board shall be in moderate contact except ... shear resistance or diaphragm action is not required.
2508.3.1	**Floating angles:** Fasteners at the top and bottom plates of vertical assemblies or the edges and ends of horizontal assemblies... are permitted to be omitted except on shear resisting elements or fire rated assemblies.
2508.5	**Horizontal gypsum board diaphragm ceilings:** Gypsum board shall be permitted to be used on wood joists to create a horizontal diaphragm ceiling in accordance with Table 2508.5.
Table 2508.5	**Allowable Shear capacity for Horizontal Wood Framed Gypsum Board Diaphragm Ceiling Assemblies**
2509	**Gypsum Board in Showers and Water Closets**
2509.2	**Base for tile:** Regular gypsum wallboard is permitted under tile or wall panels in other wall and ceiling areas when installed in accordance with GA-216 or ASTM C 840.
2509.3	**Limitations:** Water resistant gypsum backing board shall not be used in the following locations: 1 -2.
2510	**Lathing and Furring for Cement Plaster (Stucco)**
2511	**Interior Plaster**
2512	**Exterior Plaster**

Section #	Highlight
2512.1.2	**Weep screeds:** A minimum .019-inch (No. 26 galvanized sheet gauge), corrosion-resistant weep screed with a minimum vertical attachment flange… The weep screed shall be placed a minimum of 4 inches above the earth or 2 inches above paved areas and be of the type that will allow trapped water to drain to the exterior of the building.
2603	**Foam Plastic Insulation**
2603.2	**Labeling and Identification**: Packages and containers of foam plastic insulation and foam plastic insulation components delivered to the job site shall bear the label of an approved agency.
2603.4.1.5	**Roofing:** 1. The roof assembly is separated from the interior of the building by wood structural panel sheathing not less than 0.47 inch … or an equivalent material.
2611	**Light-Transmitting Plastic Skylight Glazing**
2611.3	**Slope:** Flat or corrugated light transmitting plastic skylights shall slope at least 4:12. Dome shaped skylights shall rise above the mounting flange a minimum distance equal to 10% of the max span of the dome but not less than 3 inches.
2611.5	**Aggregate area of skylights:** The aggregate area of skylights shall not exceed 33 1/3% of the floor area of the room or space sheltered by the roof for Class CC1 materials, and 25% where Class CC2 materials are utilized.
2611.6	**Separation:** Skylights shall be separated from each other by a distance of not less than 4 feet measured in a horizontal plane.
	Exceptions: 1 - 2.
Table 2902.1	**Minimum Number of Required Plumbing Fixtures**
3101.1	**Scope:** The provisions of this chapter shall govern special building construction including membrane structures … and towers and antennas. .
3103	**Temporary Structures**
3103.1.1	**Permit required:** Temporary structures that cover an area greater than 120 square feet … shall not be erected, operated or maintained for any purpose without obtaining a permit from the building official.
3103.4	**Means of egress:** Temporary structures shall conform to the means of egress requirements of Chapter 10 and shall have an exit access travel distance of 100 feet or less.
3104	**Pedestrian Walkways and Tunnels**
3105	**Awnings and Canopies**
3105.3.1	**Location**

Section #	Highlight
3105.1.1	Fabric awnings and fabric-covered frames located over public property or in areas accessible to the general public shall be constructed so that no rigid part …shall be less than 7 feet 6 inches … from the grade directly below, and no part of the cloth drop shall be less than 7 feet.
3105.4	**Design**
3105.4.2	Design of the structural framing members shall be based on rational analysis, using the applicable wind loads of Chapter 16 as shown below.
3107	**Signs**
3107.1	**General.** Signs shall be designed, constructed and in accordance with this code.
3109	**Structures Seaward of a Coastal Construction Control Line**
3109.1.1	**Scope**: The requirements of this Section 3109 do not apply to the modification … following apply to the modification, maintenance, or repair: 1-3.
3113	**Lighting, Mirrors, Landscaping**
3113.2	Each operator, or person responsible for an automated teller machine … shall provide lighting during the hours of darkness … and the exterior of and enclosed automated teller machine installation as follows: 1 - 5.
3201.4	**Drainage:** Drainage water collected from a roof, awning, canopy or marquee, and condensate from mechanical equipment shall not flow over a public walking surface.
3202	**Encroachments**
3202.2	**Encroachments above grade and below 8 feet high:** Encroachments into the public right-of-way above grade and below 8 feet in height shall be prohibited. Doors and windows shall not open or project into the public right of way.
3202.2.3	**Awnings:** The vertical clearance from the public right-of-way to the lowest part of any awning, including valances, shall not be less than 7 feet.
3202.3	**Encroachments 8 feet or more above grade:** Encroachments 8 feet or more shall comply with Sections 3202.3.1 through 3202.3.4
3202.3.1	**Awnings, canopies, marquees and signs:** Awnings, canopies, marquees and signs shall be constructed so as to support applicable loads …with less than 15 feet clearance above sidewalk shall not extend into or occupy more than two-thirds the width of the sidewalk measured from the building.
3202.3.3	**Encroachments 15 feet or more above grade:** Encroachments 15 feet or more above grade shall not be limited.
3202.4	**Temporary encroachments:** Temporary entrance awnings shall be erected with a clearance of not less than 7 feet … or approved noncombustible support.

Section #	Highlight
3303	**Demolition**
3303.1	**Construction documents:** Construction documents and a schedule for demolition ... no work until such construction documents or schedule or both are approved.
3304	**Site Work**
3304.1	**Excavation and fill:** Stumps and roots shall be removed from the soil to a depth of not less than 12 inches below the surface of the ground in the area to be occupied by the building.
3304.1.1	**Slope limits:** Slopes for permanent fill shall be not steeper than one vertical unit in two units horizontal.
3304.1.2	**Surcharge:** Existing footings or foundations which can be affected by any excavation shall be underpinned adequately or otherwise protected against settlement and shall be protected against lateral movement.
3306	**Protection of Pedestrians**
3306.2	**Walkways:** Walkways shall be sufficient width to accommodate the pedestrian traffic, but in no case shall they be less than 4 feet in width.
3306.4	**Construction Railings:** Construction Railings shall be not less than 42 inches in height and shall be sufficient to direct pedestrians around construction areas.
3306.5	**Barriers:** Barrier shall not be less than 8 feet in height and shall be placed on the side of the walkway nearest the construction.
3306.6	**Barrier Design:** Barriers shall be designed to resist loads required in Chapter 16 unless constructed as follows: 1-6.
3306.7	**Covered Walkways:** Covered walkways shall have a clear height of not less than 8 feet as measured from the floor surface to the canopy.
3308	**Temporary Use of Streets, Alleys, and Public Property**
3308.1.1	**Obstructions:** Construction materials and equipment shall not be placed or stored so as to obstruct access to fire hydrants... nor shall such material or equipment be located within 20 feet of a street intersection, or placed so as to obstruct normal observations of traffic signals or to hinder the use of public transit loading platforms.
3309	**Fire Extinguishers**
3309.1	**Where Required:** Structures under construction, alteration or demolition shall be provided with no fewer than one approved portable fire extinguisher with Section 906 and sized for not less than ordinary hazard as follows: 1-3.

1 Exam Prep
Carpentry and Building Construction Manual, 2010 Edition
Tabs and Highlights

These 1 Exam Prep Tabs are based on the *Carpentry and Building Construction Book, 2010 Edition*.

Each 1 Exam Prep Tabs sheet has five rows of tabs. Start with the first tab at the first row at the top of the page; proceed down that row placing the tabs at the locations listed below. Place each tab in your book setting it down one notch until you get to the bottom of a page. Then start back at the top again.

1 Exam Prep Tab	Page #	Highlight
Table of Contents	v	Table of Contents
Building Codes & Planning	35	Permits and Inspections
	47	Figure 2-12: Different Symbols Highlight: Brick, Concrete Block, Cinder Block and Face Grain Wood
Plans & Drawings	49	The views of a building include general drawings and detail drawings … They provide information about how parts fit together.
	50	Plan Views: Definition of site plan.
		"The basic elements of a site plan, such as the one shown in Figure 2-14, are drawn from notes and sketches based upon a survey. …This plan is used by foundation contractors."
	55	Detail Drawings: Definition of detail drawing.
		See example in Figure 2-19.
	56	Rendering: Definition of rendering. See example in Figure 2-20.
		Definition of schedule.
	57	See example in Figure 2-21.
Calculating Board Feet	63	Calculating Board Feet: Definition of board foot. See Figure 2-26.
		Rules for estimating board feet. See Table 2-3.
		Formula to determine the number of board feet in lumber.
Bar Chart	70	Bar Charts: Definition of bar chart. See example in Figure 2-28.

1 Exam Prep Tab	Page #	Highlight
Critical Path	72	Critical Path Method Diagrams: Definition of critical path method. See example in Figure 2-30.
Hand Tools	109-111	Definition and examples for:
		Try square, See Figure 4-6
		Combination square, See Figure 4-7
		Sliding T-bevel, See Figure 4-8
		Framing square, See Figure 4-9
		Triangular framing square, See Figure 4-11
		Carpenter's level, See Figure 4-12
		Torpedo level, See Figure 4-13
Concrete	218	Understanding Concrete: Definition of concrete. See concrete ingredients in Figure 8-1.
		Definition of hydration.
	221	Admixtures
	222	Definition of Super-plasticizing admixtures.
Placing Concrete	223	Working with Concrete
	226-227	Slump Testing: Definition of slump test.
		"In a slump test, concrete straight from the mixer is placed into a small sheet metal cone of specific dimensions, shown in Figure 8-5."
		"A measurement is then taken of how much the unsupported mass of concrete slumps, or looses it's conical shape, as shown in Figure 8-6."
	229	Reinforcing Bar: "Rebar comes in 20' lengths.....A rebar shear is sometimes called a rebar cutter." See example in Figure 8-9.
Site Layout	237	Site Layout
	237	Types of Instruments: Definition of laser level. See example in Figure 9-5.
	238	Definition of transit. See Figure 9-6
		Definition of vernier scale.
	239	Definition of benchmark

1 Exam Prep Tab	Page #	Highlight
	240-241	Laying out a Simple Rectangle: Steps 1-6
Locating the House on Site	243	Establishing Lines & Grades
	244	Setting up Batter Boards Steps 1-6. See Figure 9-15.
	244-245	Batter Boards: Definition of batter board.
	246	Measuring Difference in Elevation: Definition of differential leveling.
		Figure 9-17. Points visible method of measuring difference in elevation.
	249	Table 9-1: Converting Inches to Decimal Fractions of a Foot
	257	Footing Forms
	258	Definition of haunch board
		Definition of spreaders and form brackets
		"Lumber formwork is often assembled with duplex head nails to make disassembly easy later on."
	260	See Figure 10-5. "The vertical step should be poured at the same time as the rest of the footing. If the foundation wall is built with concrete block, the height of the step should be in multiples of 8". This is the height of a block with a standard 3/8" mortar joint"
		"A run is a horizontal section between two vertical sections."
		"The vertical step should be at least 6" thick and be the same width as the rest of the footing."
	262	Footing Drains: Definition of hydrostatic pressure
		Definition of foundation drains or perimeter drains
	263	"The piping can also drain into subsurface drain fields"
		"The pipes should be placed with the holes facing down." In this position, water is carried away from the house as soon as it rises into the pipes. To keep water moving, the pipes should be sloped toward the drain at least 1/8" per foot. After the pipes are in place, the drainage area should be covered with filter fabric also called (geotextile or landscaping fabric.)"

1 Exam Prep Tab	Page #	Highlight
Concrete Foundation Walls	264-265	Wall Form Details: "Wall forms may be made from wood or metal, depending on how durable they must be. Many are made from plywood and lumber. Although any exterior-grade plywood can be used, special form-grade plywood is available."
		Definition of plyform
		Definition of medium-density overlay (MDO)
		Definition of high-density overlay (HDO)
		Definition of mill-oiled plywood
		"Forms built on site may be taken apart after the concrete hardens. The lumber can then be reused elsewhere in the project. It is generally more cost effective and efficient to use reusable forms."
	268	Sill-Plate Anchors
	269	Definition of sill sealer. See example in Figure 10-12.
		Foundation Wall Details
	275	Strengthening Walls: Definition of pilaster
	277	Protecting Block Walls: "Care must be taken to keep blocks dry on the job. They should be stored on planks or other supports so the edges do not touch the ground. They should be covered for protection against moisture. Concrete block must not get wet just before or during installation."
Mortar	278	Mortar Mixtures
		Definition of Type N mortar
		Definition of Type M mortar
		Definition of Type S mortar
		Definition of Type O mortar
		Table 10-4: Proportions of Mortar Ingredients by Volume
	279	Mixing and Placing Mortar: "Mortar stiffened by hydration should be thrown away. It is not easy to tell whether evaporation or hydration is the cause."

1 Exam Prep Tab	Page #	Highlight
	279	Laying Block Foundation Walls: Building the Corners
	281	Definition of story pole or course pole. See Figure 10-28.
	285	Table: Estimating Table for Masonry Blocks
	287	Lintels and Bond Beams: Definition of lintel and the three ways to create a lintel.
		Definition of bond beam or collar beam.
Concrete Flatwork	294-295	Concrete flatwork consist of flat, horizontal areas of concrete that are usually 5" or less in thickness.
Estimating Concrete	303	Table 11-1: Estimating Materials for Concrete Slab
	304-305	Screeding: Definition of screeding. See Figure 11-11 and 11-12.
	305	Bullfloating: Definition of bullfloating. See Figure 11-13.
	306	Edging and Jointing: "When sheen has left the surface and the concrete has started to stiffen, other finishing operations can be done. Edging produces a rounded edge on the slab to prevent chipping or damage, as shown in Figure 11-14. The edger is run back and forth, covering coarse aggregate particles."
		Troweling: "For a dense, smooth finish, floating is followed by troweling with a steel trowel, as shown in Figure 11-16. For large areas, a power trowel is used instead of a hand trowel, as in Figure 11-17. Troweling cannot be started until the concrete has hardened enough to prevent fine material and water from working to the surface."
Wood as a Building Material	318-319	Wood Basics
	320	Hardwoods and Softwoods
		Table 12-1: Principal Commercial Softwoods
	324	Hardwood Grades: "Hardwood are available in three common grades, first and seconds, (FAS), select and No. 1 common."
		Figure 12-7: A Grade Stamp. Know each mark A-E.
Engineered Wood	352-353	Engineered Lumber Basics
Framing Systems	370-371	Framing Systems and Structural Design

1 Exam Prep Tab	Page #	Highlight
Floor Joist Spans	382-383	Table 14-2: Floor Joist Spans
Floor Framing	396-397	Floor Framing Basics
Dead Load Floor Joist Span	403	Table 15-2: Floor Joist Spans for Common Lumber Species
		Definition of termite shield (Box in top right corner)
	410	Bridging: "Cross bridging (also called diagonal bridging) is more common because it is very effective and requires less material. Precut 1x3 or 2x2 lumber is sometimes used for cross bridging with nailing flanges may also be used, as in Figure 15-22C."
Subfloors	421	Installing Subflooring
Wall-Framing/ Sheathing	430-431	Wall-Framing Materials
	432	Wall-Framing Members
		Studs: Definition of stud.
		Definition of king stud.
		"The use of 2 x 6 studs for exterior walls is increasingly popular. The extra thickness of the resulting wall allows space for additional insulation. These 2x6 studs may be placed 16" or 24" OC."
	434	Trimmer Studs: Definition of trimmer stud.
		Estimating Studs, Plates, and Headers: "For exterior walls with studs spaced at 16" OC, figure one stud for every lineal foot of wall. For example,… To determine the number of studs needed for a partition, refer to the table "Partition Studs Needed" in the Ready Reference Appendix."
		"To determine the number of lineal feet of top and bottom plates for walls having double top plates, multiply the length of the wall by three."
		"A rough estimate can be made as follows: 1) Figure the total length of the outside walls, and then double it…2) Multiply the total length of all walls by five…"
	435	Wall Sheathing
	440	Openings

1 Exam Prep Tab	Page #	Highlight
Calculating Door Openings	441	"Rough openings usually allow ½" on each side of the window or door and ½" at the top of the unit to allow adjustment of the unit for plumb and level installation. After you mark a window or door center-line on the plates, measure from each side of the centerline a distance equal to one half the rough opening, as shown in Figure 16-9. Now mark the plate to locate the position of each king stud."
	441	Wall Intersections: "Mark the exterior plates to indicate the centerlines of all intersecting interior walls. Again, start from one corner of the building. Mark the place where the interior wall would intersect with a P, as in Figure 16-10 on page 442."
Roof Framing	466-467	Roof Styles
Calculating Roof Slope	468-469	Calculating Roof Slope: See Figure 17-5.
	470	Definition of total run.
		Definition of unit run.
		Definition of slope.
	474	Laying Out Common Rafters
	475	Definition of theoretical length. See Figure 17-16 and 17-17.
		It may be calculated the following ways: (4 bullets)
	481	Laying Out a Bird's Mouth: Definition of bird's mouth
		Definition of heel cut
		Definition of seat cut
Basic Trusses	492-493	Roof Trusees
Hip Rafter Layout	505	Hip Rafter Layout
	507	Figure 18-5 and Figure 18-6
	550	Chimney Saddles: Definition of chimney saddle
Building a Box Cornice	556-557	Building a Box Corinice Step 1: Step 2: Step 3: Lookouts are generally made from 2 x 4 lumber. Nail through the back of the ledger into the end of each lookout with two 16d coated nails.

1 Exam Prep Tab	Page #	Highlight
		Step 4: Snap a chalk line along the length of the building on the sheathing. Step 5: Step 6: Step 7: The groove should be located about 3/8" up from the bottom edge of the fascia board. Step 8: Step 9: Nail the soffit to each lookout and to the ledger strip with 4d galvanized nails about 6" apart.
Roof Sheathing & Assembly	562-563	Roof Sheathing Spans: The stamp consists of a pair of numbers separated by a slash mark, such as 32/16 or 12/0…Note that greater spans are generally allowed for roof sheathing than for floor sheathing."
Windows & Skylights	576-577	Windows and Skylights
Residential Doors	596-597	Types of Doors
	601	Direction of Swing
	602	Figure 21-9: Door Hand. Two ways to determine the swing direction of a door.
	605	Garage Doors: "Mounting clearance required above the top of sectional overhead doors is usually about 12". However, low headroom brackets are available when such clearance is not possible. Overhead doors are usually installed by the door supplier."
	608	Preparing the Door: "When hung properly, the door should fit with an opening clearance of 1/16" at the sides and top. If the door has a sill but no threshold, the bottom clearance should be 1/16" above the sill. If it has a threshold, the bottom clearance should be 1/8" above the threshold." "Bevel the lock edge so that the inside edge will clear the jamb. This angle is about 3 degrees as shown in Figure 21-19."
	615	Interior Doors: "Most interior passage doors are 1-3/8" thick. Standard interior door height is 6'-8'. Common minimum widths for single doors are: -Bedrooms and other habitable rooms: 2'-6" -Bathrooms: 2'- 4" -Small closets and linen closets: 2'
	617	Pocket Doors: Definition of pocket door

1 Exam Prep Tab	Page #	Highlight
		"Standard widths are 2'-0", 2'-4", 2'-6", 2'-8", and 3'-0". Any style of door with a thickness of 1-3/8" can be installed in the pocket to match the other doors in the home."
	619	Installing Interior Doors: Installing the Door Frame: "Plumb the assembled frame in the rough opening using pairs of shingle shims placed between the side jambs and the studs, as in Figure 21-39."
		Hanging an Interior Door: "Interior doors are often hung with two 3-1/2" by 3-1/2" loose-pin butt hinges. However, three hinges will strengthen the door and help to prevent it from warping."
	620	Door Stops and Trim: "After the door is in place, permanently nail the stops with 1-1/2" finish nails. Nail the stop on the lock side first, setting it tightly against the door face while the door is latched. Space the nails 16" apart in pairs. Nail the stop behind the hinge side next. Allow a 1/32" clearance from the door face to prevent scraping as the door is opened as shown in Figure 21-42".
Roofing & Gutters	626-627	Roofing Terms and Concepts: Definition of square
		Definition of coverage
	629	Roll Roofing
Underlayment/ Flashing	632	Installation Materials: Definition of underlayment
		Four purposes of underlayment
	633	Flashing: "Eaves protection should extend from the end of the eaves to a point at least 22" inside the exterior wall line of the house, as in Figure 22-11."
		"Flashing must be installed so that it sheds water. Metal used for flashing must be corrosion resistant. Galvanized steel (at least 26 gauge), 0.019" thick aluminum, 16 oz. copper, or lead-coated copper can be used."
	634	Drip Edge: Definition of drip edges
	636	Installing Underlayment: "Make sure to create a top lap of at least 2" at all horizontal joints and a 4" side lap at all end joints. Lap the underlayment over all hips and ridges for 6" on each side."
Laying Shingles	637	Laying Shingles
	638	Two methods for alignment are: -Method 1: Breaking the joints on halves -Method 2: Breaking the joints on thirds

1 Exam Prep Tab	Page #	Highlight
		Nailing: "Nails should be made of hot-dipped galvanized steel, aluminum, or stainless steel. A roofing nail has a sharp point and a large, flat head at least 3/8" in diameter. Shanks should be 10-to 12-gauge wire."
		"In areas where high, local codes may require six nails per shingle…To provide extra resistance to uplift in high wind areas, use six nails for each strip."
	642	Table 22-1: Determining Roof Area from a Plan
	651	Gutter Systems
	652	Installation: "To ensure the correct slope, measure the distance in feet from one end of the fascia to the other. Round up to the nearest whole foot. Multiply this number by 1/16".
Siding	658-659	Types of wood Siding
	660-661	Flashing: "Metal flashing is used to seal the joints where the siding meets a horizontal surface…Flashing should extend well under the siding and sufficiently over ends of a well-sloped drip cap to prevent water from seeping in." See Figure 23-3.
	661	Protecting the Sheathing: Definition of housewrap.
Brick Masonry	690-691	Brick Basics
Mortar Basics	694	Definition of Type M mortar
		Definition of Type S mortar
		Definition of Type N mortar
		Definition of Type O mortar
Brick Veneer	697	Figure 24-12 and Figure 24-13
	698	Flashing and Drainage: Definition of weep hole How weep holes are formed
		Wall Ties: Definition of wall ties
		Figure 24-14: Various types of wall ties

1 Exam Prep Tab	Page #	Highlight
Estimating Brick	702	Estimating Brick: "A Rough estimate of bricks needed may be made based on a wall's square footage. Approximately seven standard bricks are needed for every square foot of veneer wall. This includes a small allowance for waste. After calculating the square footage of walls, minus any openings, multiply this figure by 7 to get the number of bricks required. Another method is to consult Table 24-2."
Fireplace & Chimneys	704-705	Fireplace and Chimneys
	706	Hearth: Definition of hearth.
		Two parts of a hearth and requirements.
	711-712	Chimney Construction Details: Flue Liners: Definition of flue liners.
	714	Definition of saddle (chimney cricket) and building code requirements. See example of saddle in Figure 24-31.
Stairways	724-725	Parts of a Stairway
	726	Definition of stringer
		Definition of balusters
	726-727	Handrails and Balusters
	728	Definition of gooseneck
	729	Definition of newel
		Definition of landing newel/starting newel
		Definition of angle newel
		Stairway Planning
	730	Definition of winders
Stairway Calculations	734	Calculating Total Run: Definition of total run
		Figure 25-12: Methods Used to Anchor the Stringers
		Calculating Unit Rise and Run (Steps 1-5)
Molding & Trim	750-751	Molding & Trim Basics
	752	Figure 26-3: Typical Molding Profiles

1 Exam Prep Tab	Page #	Highlight
Door & Window Details	759	Door Casing
	760-761	Window Casing and Shutters: Definition of stool
		Definition of apron
		See example of stool and apron in Figure 26-14
		"The window stool is normally the first piece of window trim to be installed. It is notched so that it fits between the jambs and butts against the lower sash. Refer to Figure 26-15. The upper drawing shows the stool in place. The lower drawing shows it laid out and cut, ready for installation."
Cabinets & Countertops	780-781	Planning for Cabinets
	783-784	"Wall cabinets are usually 12" deep and are often located beneath a soffit.
		Definition of soffit.
Insulation/R-Value	894-895	Definition of R-value
		Table 31-1: Thermal Properties of various Building Material per Inch of Thickness
	900	Controlling Moisture: Definition of condensation and example.
	901	Attic Ventilation
	902	"Where a sloped ceiling is insulated, there should be a free opening of at least 1-1/2" between the sheathing and the insulation to encourage are movement."
	906	See "Job Safety" Box: Handling Fiberglass
Suspended Ceiling	938-939	Installing a Suspended Ceiling (Steps 1-7)
	941	Acoustical Ceilings: Definition of Acoustical Ceiling
Finish Flooring	972-973	Wood Flooring Basics
	975	Storage and Handling of Wood Flooring: "Never unload wood flooring when it is raining or snowing...Never store wood flooring directly in contact with a concrete floor."
Laying Tongue & Groove	979	Laying Strip Flooring

1 Exam Prep
OSHA 29 CFR 1926
Tabs and Highlights

These 1 Exam Prep Tabs are based on the *29 CFR 1926 OSHA Construction Industry Regulations*.

Each Tabs sheet has five rows of tabs. Start with the first tab at the first row at the top of the page; proceed down that row placing the tabs at the locations listed below. Place each tab in your book setting it down one notch until you get to the last tab (usually the index or glossary). Then start with the highlights.

*Note: In the July 2014 and January 2015 Edition, Section 1910 is located at the front of the book, in numerical order. In the July 2015 Edition, Section 1910 is located throughout the book and is *not* in numerical order. You will need to use the index and/or table of contents in the book to locate the page numbers for the highlights and/or tabs for Section 1910. This is excellent practice for your exam.

*Note: Section 1926 is located in all OSHA editions in numerical order. Page numbers are not provided since the edition changes every six (6) months.

1 Exam Prep Tab	Section #
Table of Contents	i
1903: Inspections	1903.3
Citations/Penalties	1903.14
1904: Recordkeeping	1904.0
Fatalities	1904.39
1910: General	1910.12
Escape Only Respirators	1910.134
QLFT	1910.134
*Permit Required Spaces	1910.146
Lockout Tagout	1910.147
Access to Records	1910.1020
Noise Exposure	1926.52
Hazard Communications	1910.1200
Personal & Life Saving Equipment	Subpart E
Fire Protection & Prevention	Subpart F

This Tab only appears in editions prior to July 2015

New Tab 04/27/16. If you have purchased pre-printed tabs please write this one in.

1 Exam Prep Tab	Section #
Yard Storage	1926.151(C) *New Tab 04/27/16. If you have purchased pre-printed tabs please write this one in.*
Signs, Signals & Barricades	Subpart G
Material Handling, Storage Use & Disposal	Subpart H
Tools - Hand & Power	Subpart I
Compressed Air	1926.302(b)(4)
Welding & Cutting "Cracking"	Subpart J
Electrical	Subpart K
Scaffolds	Subpart L
Fall Protection	Subpart M
Roof Widths	1926.501 (b)(10)
Personal Fall Systems	1926.502(d)
Positioning Device Systems	1926.502(e)
Sample Fall Protection	1926.502(k)
Cranes, Derricks & Hoists	Subpart N
Motor Vehicles	Subpart O
Excavations	Subpart P
Soil Classifications	Appendix A
Sloping & Benching	Appendix B
Demolition	Subpart T
Power & Distribution	Subpart V
Rollover & Overhead Protection	Subpart W
Stairways & Ladders	Subpart X
Diving	Subpart Y

1 Exam Prep Tab	Section #
Toxic & Hazardous Substances	Subpart Z
Index	Index

This concludes the tabs for this document. Please continue with the highlights on the following page.

Section #	Highlight
1903	**Inspections, Citations, and Proposed Penalties**
1904.1	**Recording and Reporting Occupational Injuries and Illnesses**
1904.1(a)(1)	**Basic Requirement:** If your company had ten (10) or fewer employees at all times during the last calendar year, you do not need to keep OSHA illness and injury records.
1904.39	**Reporting fatalities and multiple hospitalization incidents to OSHA**
1910	**General Industry Standards**
1910.134(b)	Escape only respirators means a respirator intended to be used only for emergency exist.
1910.134(f)(6)	QLFT may only be used to fit test negative pressure air purifying respirators that must achieve a fit factor of 100 or less.
1910.146	**Permit required confined spaces**
1910.147	**The control of hazardous energy (lockout/tagout)**
1910.1020	**Access to employee exposure and medical records**
1910.1020(e)(1)(i)	Whenever an employee requests access to records (15 days)
1910.1200	**Hazard Communications**
Subpart A	**General**
1926.1	**Purpose and scope**
1926.3	**Right of Entry, right to accompany**
Subpart B	**General Interpretations**
1926.12	Reconciles various documents and Acts
1926.13	**Interpretation of Statutory Terms**

Section #	Highlight
1926.15(b)	Federal Contracts over $10,000: Nothing can be bought from violating manufacturer's; no services from violating contractors
Subpart C	**General Safety and Health provisions**
1926.20 (a)(1)	**General safety and health provisions.** No one works in unsafe environment
	1926.21(b)(2) Employer responsibility: instruct each employee in the recognition and avoidance of unsafe conditions
1926.21-31	First aid, fire, housekeeping, illumination, sanitation, personal protective equipment, these are all general areas of employer responsibility. Specific details are not elaborated in the remainder of 1926
1926.32(d)	Definition of an authorized person
1926.32(m)	Definition of a qualified person
1926.32(j)	Definition of an employee
Subpart D	**Occupational Health and Environmental Controls** – minimum site conditions
1926.50	**First Aid Kits (Non-Mandatory)**
1926.51	**Sanitation.** Potable water available. See Table D-1 for number of employees and minimum # of facilities
1926.52	**Occupational noise exposure.** Table D-2 Permissible noise exposures. The info from the table is used to complete the formula under it. If after the calculation is done, the answer exceeds 1 (unity) it means that the cumulative effect of long term exposure equals to lower levels of noise or exceeds the limit of exposure and therefore has the effect of injury.
1926.55	**Vapors, fumes, dusts, and mists. Appendix A-1970 American Conference of Governmental Hygienists' Threshold Limit Values of Airborne Contaminants**
1926.56	**Illumination: Table D-3 Minimum Illumination Intensities in Foot Candles**
1926.57	**Ventilation.** This section covers grinding or dust and particle producing activities, such as abrasive blasting grinding, polishing equipment.
1926.60	**Methylenedianiline.** Practices and procedures for Methylenedianiline.
1926.62	**Lead**. References Appendix A-D; Begins section on lead, Lead paint reduction, protection esp. PEL 50 micrograms per cubic meter of air.
1926.62(f)	**Respiratory Protection**

Section #	Highlight
1926.62(j)(2)	**Biological monitoring**
1926.64	**Process safety management of highly hazardous chemicals.**
Subpart E	**Personal & Life Saving Equipment**
1926.95	**Criteria for personal protective equipment.** Section starts identifying and prescribing head, hearing, eye and face protection measures. Shall be provided; employer responsible that equipment is safe design and use head protection whenever necessary
1926.100	**Head Protection**
1926.102	**Eye and Face Protection**
1926.104	**Safety belts, lifelines, and lanyards.** Safety belts, minimum 5,400 dead weight, 1/2 inch thick nylon, hardware cadmium plated type 1 class b plating, tensile loading 4,000 lbs
1926.105	**Safety Nets.** Safety nets, needed over 25', 6" x 6" mesh, 17500 foot points minimum resistance; edge ropes 5000
1926.106	**Working over or near water.** Over water: Ring buoys 90 feet line, 200 max distance.
Subpart F	**Fire Protection and Prevention**
1926.150	**Fire protection. Table F-1 Fire Extinguishers Data**
1926.151	**Fire prevention**
1926.151(C)	**Open Yard Storage**
1926.152	**Flammable liquids**
1926.153	**Liquefied Petroleum Gas (LP-Gas).** Includes handling and storage as well as container. Specifications, Table F-3 & F-31 Storage of LP-gas.
1926.154	Table F-4 minimum clearance for heating equipment.
Subpart G	**Signs, Signals and Barricades**
1926.200	**Accident prevention signs and tags.** Accident prevention, danger and caution defined. Specific coloring; exit, safety instruction, directional traffic signs defined, accident prevention tags demonstrated
Subpart H	**Material Handling, Storage Use & Disposal**
1926.250	**Requirements for storage**

Section #	Highlight
1926.250(b)	**Material storage.** (1) "Material stored inside buildings under construction shall not be placed within 6 feet of any hoist way or inside floor openings …"(4) "Bagged materials shall be stacked by stepping back the layers and cross keying the bags at least every 10 bags high."(6) "Brick stacks not more than 7' in height. When a loose brick reaches a height of 4', it shall be tapered back 2" per ft. the above 4' level." (7) When masonry blocks are stacked higher than 6', the stack shall be tapered back ½ block per tier above the 6' level." (8) Lumber.
1926.251	**Rigging equipment and material handling.**
1926.251(c)	(4)(iv) Wire rope shall not be used if any length of eight diameters, 10% strands broken (13) Minimum sling lengths 10 times component rope diameter (14) Safe operating temperatures
1926.251(d)	Natural ropes and synthetic fiber. (2)(i) In manila rope, eye splices shall contain at least three full tucks. (2)(iii) strand end tails various minimums (6) Removal from service
	Tables H-1 through H-2. Series of tables for capacities for various slings
1926.252	**Disposal of Waste Materials**
Subpart I	**Tools -Hand & Power**
1926.300	**General Requirements.** Various rules about specific tools and machines.
1926.300(b)(4)(iv).	"The following are some machines which usually require point of operation guarding: (Note [a]-[i])."
1926.300(d)	**Switches**
1926.301	**Hand Tools.** Various rules of operation for powerhand tools
1926.302	**Power-operated Hand Tools**
1926.302(b)(4)	"Compressed air should not be used for cleaning purposes except where reduced to less than 30 psi and then only with effective chip guarding and personal protective equipment which meets the requirements the requirements of subpart E of this part…"
1926.303	**Abrasive wheels and tools**
1926.303(b)(1)	**Guarding.** Grinding machines shall be equipped with safety guards.
1926.304	**Woodworking Tools**
1926.305	**Jacks – lever and ratchet, screw, and hydraulic.** Blocking required for firm foundation
Subpart J	**Welding & Cutting**

Section #	Highlight
1926.350	**Gas welding and cutting**
1926.350(a)	**Transporting, moving, and storing compressed gas cylinders.**
1926.350(a)(10)	Oxygen cylinders in storage shall be separated from fuel-gas cylinders … having a fire resistance rating of at least one-half hour.
1926.350(d)	**Use of Fuel Gas**. The employer shall thoroughly instruct employees in the safe use of fuel gas, as follows:
1926.350(d)(1)	Before a regulator to a cylinder valve is connected … This action is general termed "cracking" and is intended to clear the valve of dust or dirt that might otherwise enter the regulator.)
1926.351	**Arc Welding and Cutting**
1926.351(d)	**Operating Instructions**. Employers shall instruct employees in the safe means of arc welding and cutting as follows:
1926.351(d)(1)	When electrode holders are left unattended … with employees or conducting objects.
1926.354	**Welding, cutting, and heating in way of preservative coatings.** (a) "Before welding cutting or heating is commenced on any surface covered by a preservative coating whose flammability is unknown, a test shall be made by a competent person to determine its flammability."
Subpart K	**Electrical**
1926.400	**Installation Safety Requirements Introduction**
1926.403	**General Requirements: Tables K-1 Working Clearances, K-2: Minimum Depth of Clear Working Space, K-3 Elevation of Unguarded Energized Parts**
1926.404	**Wiring design and protection.**
1926.404(b)	**Branch Circuits**
1926.404(b)(1)	Ground-fault protection
1926.404(b)(1)(ii)	Ground-fault circuit interrupters. All 120-volt, single-phase, 15- and 20-ampere receptacle outlets … need not be protected with ground-fault circuit interrupters.
	[C] Each chord set, attachment cap, plug and receptacle ... Equipment fund damaged or defective shall not be used until repaired.
	[D] The following tests shall be performed on all cord sets … [1] – [2].
1926.404(b)(2)	**Table K-4: Receptacle Ratings for Various Size Circuits**

Section #	Highlight
1926.405	**Wiring Methods, Components, and Equipment for General Use**
1926.407	**Hazardous locations**. Section deals with classification of locations from Class I – III
1926.408	**Special Systems**
Subpart L	**Scaffolds**
1926.450	**Scope, application, and definitions applicable to this subpart.**
1926.450(b)	**Definitions**
1926.451	**General Requirements**
1926.451(a)	**Capacity.** (1) scaffold component shall be capable of supporting, without failure, its own weight and at least support 4 times the maximum intended load. (2) Direct connections to roofs and floors, and counterweights … at least 4 times the tipping moment.(3) Each suspension rope … at least 6 times the maximum intended load.(4) Each suspension rope … 6 times intended load … or 2 (minimum) times the stall load of the hoist, whichever is greater. (5) Stall load not exceed 3 times rated load (6) Scaffolds shall be designed by a qualified person … Non-mandatory Appendix A to this subpart contains examples of criteria that will enable the employer to comply with paragraph (a) of this section.
1926.451(b)	**Scaffold platform construction**. (1)Each platform on all working levels of scaffolds shall be fully planked or decked between the front uprights and guardrail supports as follows: (i) Each platform unit … uprights is no more than 1 inch wide (ii) Where the employer makes demonstration …remaining open space between the platform and the uprights shall not exceed 9 1/2 inches (2) Except provided in paragraphs … at least 18 inches wide (i) Each ladder jack scaffold... at least 12 inches wide (ii) Where scaffolds must be used … 18 inches wide… personal fall arrest systems. (3) Except as provided …the front edge of all platforms shall not be more than 14" from the face of the work … of this section to protect an employee from falling. (i) The maximum distance from the face for outrigger scaffolds shall be 3 inches. (ii) The maximum distance from the face for plastering and lathing operations shall be 18 inches. (4) Each end of a platform...extend over the centerline of its support at least 6 inches. (5)(i) Each end of a platform 10 feet or less in length shall not extend over its support more than 12 inches … or has guardrails which block employee access. (ii) Each platform greater than 10 feet in length shall not extend more than 18 inches … or has guardrails which block employee access to cantilevered ends.
1926.451(c)	**Criteria for supported scaffolds**. (1) "Supported scaffolds with height to base width ratio of more than four to one (4:1) shall be restrained…"
1926.451(d)	**Criteria for Suspension Scaffolds**

Section #	Highlight
1926.451(e)	**Access.** This paragraph applies to .... (1) "When scaffold platforms are more than 2 feet above or below a point of access, portable ladders, hook-on ladders, attachable ladders, stair towers, stairway-type ladders, ramps, walkways, integral prefabricated scaffold access, or direct access from another scaffold ,,, shall be used." (3)"Stairway-type ladders shall: (i) - (iii)." (4) "Stair towers shall be positioned such that their bottom step is not more than 23 inches above the scaffold supporting level."
1926.451 (g)	**Fall protection**. (1) Each employee on a scaffold more than 10 feet above a lower level shall be protected from falling to that lower level. (iii) Each employee on a crawling board ... minimum 200 lb top rail capacity ... handhold securely fastened beside each crawling board. (3) In addition to meeting the requirements of ... adjustable suspension scaffold. (ii) When horizontal lifelines are used, they shall be secured to two or more structural members of the scaffold ... Horizontal lifelines shall not be attached only to suspension ropes. (4) Guardrail systems installed ... meet the requirements of paragraphs (g)(4) (vii), (viii), and (ix) of this section. (vii) Each top rail or equivalent ...100 pounds for guard-rail systems installed on single-point ... or two-point adjustable ... at least 200 pounds for guardrail systems installed on other scaffolds. (viii) When loads specified ... shall not drop below the height above the platform surface ... of this section.
1926.451(h)	**Falling object protection.**(2)Where there is danger of tools ... the following provisions apply: (ii) A toe board shall be erected along the edge of platforms more than 10 feet above lower levels ... wood or equivalent may be used in lieu of toeboards. (4) Where used, toeboards shall be:(ii) At least three and one-half inches high from the top edge of the toe board to the level of the working surface ... Toeboads shall be solid or with openings not over one inch in the greatest dimension.
1926.452	**Additional Requirements for specific types of scaffolding** (a) Pole Scaffolding (b) Tube and coupler scaffolds (c) Fabricated frame scaffolds (6)Scaffolds over 125 feet in height above their base shall be designed by a registered engineer (d) Plasterer's scaffolding (e) Bricklayer's square scaffolds (f) Horse scaffolds (g) Form and carpenter's bracket (h) Roof bracket scaffolds (j) Pump jack scaffold (k) Ladder jack scaffold (1) Window jack scaffold (m) Crawling boards (chicken ladders) (n) Step platform and trestle ladder (o) Single point adjustable suspension (p) Two point adjustable suspension (q) Multi point adjustable (r) Catenary (s) Float (ship)

Section #	Highlight
	(t) Interior hung (u) Needle beam (v) Multi-level suspended (w) Mobile (x) Repair bracket scaffolds (y) Stilts
1926.453	**Aerial Lifts**
1926.454	**Training Requirements**
Appendix A	**Scaffold Specifications (Non-mandatory). Index to Appendix A for Subpart L**. Note: This is indicating where more detail can be found for scaffolding which was defined above. Two tables, first maximum intended nominal load (this table correlates load with thickness for dressed and undressed lumber rated capacity).
Appendix E	Pictorial of types of scaffolding components and basic rules identified.
Subpart M	**Fall Protection**
1926.500	**Scope, application, and definitions applicable to this subpart.**
1926.500(b)	**Definitions**
1926.501(b)(10)	Determining Roof Widths
1926.501	**Duty to have fall protection**
1926.501(b)	(1) Unprotected sides above 6' must have guard rail (2) Leading edge above 6 feet guardrail, or safety net, or personal protection required (above 6' is key) (10) Roofing work on low slope system requires warning line or guard rail, or safety net, or personal fall arrest system: exception width 50' or less can use safety monitoring system
1926.501(c)	**Protection from falling objects**: "when an employee is exposed to falling objects, the employer shall have each employee wear a hard hat and shall implement one of the following measures: 1. Erect toe boards; 2. Erect a canopy structure; 3. Barricade
1926.502	**Fall protection systems criteria and practices**
1926.502(b)	**Guardrail systems.** (1) Top edge height 42 inches plus or minus 3"(2) Midrails, screens, mesh...installed between the top edge of the guardrail system and the walking surface... when there is no wall or parapet wall at least 21 inches high (iv) ...no openings in the guardrail system that are more than 19 inches wide (4) Guardrail systems capable... 200 lbs applied within 2 inches of the top edge (9) Top rails and midrails shall be at least 1/4" nominal diameter or thickness to prevent cuts
1926.502(c)	**Safety net systems.** (1) Safety nets.... no case more than 30 feet below such level(2) Safety nets shall extend outward

Section #	Highlight
1926.502(d)	**Personal fall arrest systems.** Body belts not acceptable (9) Lanyards a vertical lifelines shall have a minimum breaking strength of 5,000lbs (12) Self retracting lifelines... limit free fall distance to 2 ft. with minimum tensile load of 3,000lbs (15) Anchorages used for...personal fall arrest equipment.... 5,000lbs (16) (system) shall: (i) limit arresting force on employee to 900lbs with body belt (ii) 1,800 lbs with body harness (iii) employee can neither free fall more than 6', (iv) deceleration distance limited to 3.5 feet (v) Have sufficient strength to withstand twice the potential impact energy of an employee free falling a distance of 6'.
1926.502(e)	**Positioning device system** (1) Positioning device systems...shall be rigged such that an employee cannot free fall more than 2' (2) Positioning devices....load...3,000 lbs (5)Connecting assemblies 5,000lbs (6) dee rings, snaphooks,3600 lbs
1926.502(f)	**Warning line systems**. (2)(i) Flagged at 6' intervals (2)(ii) Lowest point 34", highest 39" (2)(iii) Tipping 16 lbs (iv) Rope, 500lbs
1926.502(g)	**Controlled access zones** This section defines storage areas, cover controls and stacking materials. Fall protection plan defined as option.
1926.502(k)	Sample Fall Protection Plan
1926.503	**Training Requirements**
Subpart N	**Cranes, Derricks & Hoists**
1926.551	**Helicopters**
1926.552	**Material Hoists, Personnel elevators**
1926.552(b)	**Material hoists.** (2) Entryways protected by 2x4 bars 2' from hoistway line, not less than 36 nor more than 42 inches above floor.
1926.552(c)	**Personnel hoists.** (3) Towers shall be anchored ...not exceeding 25'(14) Note the table titled, **Minimum Factors of Safety for Suspension Wire Ropes**
1926.553	**Base Mounted drum hoists**
1926.554	**Overhead Hoists**
1926.555	**Conveyors**
Subpart O	**Motor Vehicles and Marine Operations**
1926.600	**Equipment**
1926.602	**Material Handling Equipment**

Section #	Highlight
1926.603	**Pile driving equipment**
1926.605	**Marine Operations and Equipment**
Subpart P	**Excavations**
1926.650	**Scope application, and definitions applicable to this subpart.** (For additional reference see Walkers Builder's Estimators Reference Table B4 if your exam calls for this book.)
1926.651	**Specific excavation requirements**
1926.651(c)	**Access and egress.** (2)Means of egress needed at depth 4' or over
1926.651(g)	**Hazardous atmospheres.** (1)(i) *"Where oxygen deficiency* (atmospheres containing less than 19.5 percent oxygen) or a hazardous atmosphere exists or could reasonably be expected to exist, such as in excavations in landfill areas or excavations in areas where hazardous substances are stored nearby, the excavations greater than 4 feet in depth."
1926.651(i)	**Stability of adjacent structures.**
1926.651(j)	**Protection of employees from loose rock or soil.** (2) *"Employees shall be protected from excavated or other materials* or equipment that could pose a hazard by falling or rolling into excavations. Protection shall be3 provided by placing and keeping such materials or equipment at least 2 feet from the edge of excavations, or by the use of retaining devices that are sufficient to prevent materials or equipment from falling …"
1926.652	**Requirements for protective systems**
1926.652(b)	**Design of sloping and benching systems.** (1) Option 1 allowable configurations and slopes (2) Option 2 determination of slopes and configurations using appendices A and B (3) Designs using other tabulated data (4) Design by a registered professional engineer
Subpart P	**Appendix A: Soil Classification.** This section provides definitions, including types A, B & C soil *"Type A* means cohesive soils with an unconfined compressive strength of 1.5 ton per square foot (tsf) or greater. Examples of cohesive soils are: clay, silty clay, sandy clay, clay loam …" *"Type B* means: (i) *Cohesive soil with an unconfined* compressive strength greater than .05 tsf but less than 1.5 tsf …" *"Type C* means: (i) *Cohesive soil with an unconfined* compressive strength of 0.5 tsf or less …"

Section #	Highlight

Subpart P — **Appendix B: Sloping and Benching.** This section provides pictorial descriptions of run to rise calculations. Also Figure B-1 which relates the types of soil to the required run to rise (horizontal to vertical) ratio to determine the amount of slope.

(b) **Definitions**. "*Distress* means that the soil is in a condition where a cave-in is imminent or is likely to occur. Distress is evidenced by such phenomena as the development of fissures in the face of adjacent to an open excavation; the subsidence of the edge of an excavation; the slumping of material from the face or the bulging or heaving of material …"

(3) *Actual Slope.* (ii) "*The actual slope shall be less* steep than the maximum allowable slope, when there are signs of distress. If that situation occurs, the slope shall be cut back to an actual slope which is at least 1/2 horizontal to one vertical (1/2 H:1V) less steep than the maximum allowable slope."

(4)"*Configurations.*" Configurations of sloping and benching systems shall be in accordance with Figure B-1." Note: **Figure B-1** and number 3 in the notes.

Subpart P — **Appendix C:** Tables **C-1.1** through **C-2.3**

Appendix D: Tables **D-1.1** through **D-1.4** These are aluminum shoring components flow charts.

Subpart Q — **Concrete and Masonry Construction**

1926.700 — **Scope, application, and definitions applicable to this subpart.**

1926.700(b) — **Definitions** 1 – 9.

1926.702(b) — **Concrete mixers.** Concrete mixers with 1 c.y. or more shall be equipped with: (1) Mechanical device to clear the skip; (2) Guardrails installed

1926.702(c) — **Power concrete trowels.** Shall be equipped with a control switch that will automatically shut off the power whenever the hands of the operator are removed … handles.

1926.702(j) — **Lockout / tag out procedures**

1926.703 — **Requirements for cast in place concrete**

1926.703(b) — **Shoring and Reshoring**

1926.704 — **Requirements for precast concrete**

1926.706 — **Requirements for masonry construction**

1926.706 (a) — **A limited access zone shall be established** … shall conform to the following:

Section #	Highlight
1926.706(b)	**All masonry walls over 8 ft. in height** shall be adequately braced to prevent overturning … elements of the structure are in place.
Subpart R	**Steel Erection**
1926.751	**Definitions**
1926.754	**Structural steel assembly**
1926.754 (b)	**The following additional requirements** shall apply for multi-story structures. (2) At no time shall there be more than four floors or 48 feet of unfinished bolting … result of the design.
Subpart S	**Underground Construction, Caissons, Cofferdams and Compressed Air**
1926.800	**Underground Construction**
1926.802	**Cofferdams**
1926.803	**Compressed air**
Subpart T	**Demolition**
1926.850	**Preparatory operations**
1926.851	**Stairs, passageways and ladders**
1926.852	**Chutes**
1926.852(b)	"The openings shall not exceed 48 inches in height measured along the wall of the chute."
1926.859	**Mechanical demolition**
1926.859(b)	"**The weight of the ball** shall not exceed 50 % or the cranes rated load…"
Subpart U	**Blasting and Use of Explosives**
Subpart V	**Power Transmissions and Distribution**
1926.965	**Underground Electrical Installations**
1926.968	**Definitions:** barrier and barricade
Subpart W	**Rollover Protective Structures; Overhead Protection**
Subpart X	**Stairways and Ladders**

Section #	Highlight
1926.1050	**Scope, application, and definitions applicable to this subpart**
1926.1050(b)	**Definitions**
1926.1051	**General Requirements**
1926.1051(a)	Needed break in elevation of 19 inches (1) No spiral staircases unless permanent ones (2) Double cleated ladder or two or more separate ladders provided... 25 employees or more
1926.1052	**Stairways**
1926.1052(a)	(1) Landings not less than 30 inches and extend 22 inches (3) Variations in riser height and tread depth not over 1/4"
1926.1052(c)	**Stair-rails and handrails**
	(1) Stairways having four or more risers, or rising more than 30 inches … shall be equipped with (i) At least one handrail (ii) One stairrail system along each unprotected side or edge
	(4)(11) Handrails that will not be permanent … minimum clearance of 3 inches … and other objects.
1926.1053	**Ladders**
1926.1053(a)	(1) Ladders shall be capable of supporting the following loads without failure: (i) Each self-supporting potable ladder ... sustain at least 3.3 times the max. intended load … appendix A of this subpart will be deemed to meet this requirement. (ii) Each portable ladder that is not self-supporting: At least four times the maximum intended load … appendix A will be deemed to meet this requirement. (iii) Each fixed ladder: At least two loads of 250 pounds each ... appendix A will be deemed to meet this requirement (3)(i) Rungs, cleats and steps of portable ladders and fixed shall be spaced not less than 10 inches nor more than 14 inches apart. (3)(ii) Rungs, cleats and steps of step stools not less than 8 inches apart, nor more than 12 inches … as measured between center lines of the rungs, cleats, and steps. (3)(iii) Rungs, cleats and steps of … trestle ladders not less than 8 inches nor more than 18 inches …as measured between center lines of the rungs, cleats, and steps. (4)(i) The minimum clear distance between sides of individual ladders... shall be 16 inches. (6)(i) The rungs of fixed metal ladders … treated to minimize slipping. (7) Ladders shall not be tied or fastened together … unless they are specifically designed for such use. (8) A metal spreader or locking device shall be provided on each step ladder … when the ladder is being used.

Section #	Highlight
	(13) The minimum perpendicular clearance fixed ladder rungs, cleats, and steps 4.5 … inches where required. (19)Where the total length of a climb equals or exceeds 24 feet the following applies: (i-iii) (21) Wells for fixed ladders shall conform to all of the following: (i-v) (22) Ladder safety devices … shall conform to all of the following: (i-iv) (24) The side rails of a through or side step fixed ladder shall extend 42 inches above the top of the access level … the top of the parpet.
1926.1053(b)	**Use.** (1)"When portable ladders are used for access to an upper landing surface, the ladder side rails shall extend at least 3'...(5)(i) Non Self supporting ....used at an angle such that horizontal distance from the top support to the foot of the ladder is approx. 1/4 the working length of the ladder (5)(ii) Wood job made ladders with spliced side rails shall be used at an angle ...1/8 working length
Subpart Y	**Diving**
1926.1091	Record Keeping Requirements
Subpart Z	**Toxic and Hazardous Substances**
1926.1101	**Asbestos**
1926.1101(b)	**Definitions**
1926.1101(c)	**Permissible exposure limits (PELS).** (1) *"Time-weighted average limit (TWA).* The employer shall ensure that no employee is exposed to an airborne concentration of asbestos in excess of 0.1 fiber per cubic centimeter of air as an eight hour time-weighted average … or by an equivalent method."
1926.1101(g)	**Methods of compliance.** (8) *Additional Controls for Class II work.* (i) *"For removing vinyl and asphalt flooring materials* … these practices pursuant to paragraph (k)(9)" (ii) *"For removing roofing materials* … the following work practices are followed" (iii) *"When removing cementitious asbestos-containing* siding and shingles … the following work practices are followed" (iv) *"When removing gaskets containing ACM* … the following work practices are followed" (v) *"When performing any other Class II removal* of asbestos containing material for which specific controls have not been listed … the following work practices are complied with." (vi) *"Alternative Work Practices and Controls* … the following provisions are complied with.*"
1926.1101(h)	**Respirator protection.** (ii) Employers must provide an employee with … PAPR and it provides adequate protection to the employee. (iii) Employers must provide employees with an air-purifying half mask … whenever employees perform:

Section #	Highlight
1926.1101(j)	**Hygiene facilities and practices for employees**. (1) Requirements for employees performing Class I … surfacing ACM and PACM.(i) "*Decontamination areas …* regulated through the decontamination area. [A] Equipment room [B] Shower area [C] Clean change room.
Subpart CC	**Cranes and Derricks in Construction**
1926.1400	**Scope**
1926.1401	**Definitions**
1926.1412	**Inspections**
1926.1415	**Safety devices**
1926.1417	**Operation**
1926.1419	**Signals - general requirements**
1926.1423	**Fall protection**
1926.1431	**Hoisting personnel**
1926.1435	**Tower cranes**
1926.1436	**Derricks**
1926.1437	**Floating cranes/derricks and land cranes/derricks on barges**
1926.1438	**Overhead & gantry cranes**
Index	**Index**
Inside back cover	Examples of OSHA reporting forms 300 and 300a, how to fill them out and summary of when required.

1 Exam Prep
OSHA - (29 CFR PART 1926)
Questions and Answers

1. The ratio of the ultimate breaking strength of a piece of equipment to the actual working stress when in use is known as the _____ .

A. occupational hazard
B. construction condition
C. condition of protection
D. safety factor

A female employee complains that there are not separate toilets for the 20 women working on the site. She further states that all 160 males and females use the same toilet. She said that the contractor is not complying with OSHA. According to OSHA, the employee_____ .

A. does not have a valid complaint since OSHA has no specific instructions as to male and female toilets. The project is only required to have four toilets and four urinals.
B. does not have a valid complaint since OSHA has no specific instructions as to male and female toilets. The project is only required to have five toilets and five urinals.
C. has a valid complaint since OSHA specifies that five toilets and five urinals for men and a separate toilet for women are required on a project of that size.
D. has a valid complaint since OSHA specifies five toilets and four urinals for men and a separate toilet for women are required on a project of that size.

3. A first aid kit must be checked _____ .

A. daily   B. weekly   C. monthly   D. annually

4. Potable drinking water, per OSHA requires:

A. if a container is used it must have a tap.
B. a common drinking cup is allowed if washed.
C. single serving cups do not have to be provided.
D. open containers can be used if single serving cups are provided.

5. One toilet shall be provided at the construction job site for maximum of _____ employees.

A. 5   B. 10   C. 15.   D. 20

6. Given the following: 1-1/2 hr noise exposure at 90 dBA 1/2

                    hr noise exposure at 100 dBA

                    1/2 hr noise exposure at 105 dBA

If your employees are exposed to all of the above noise levels each work day, then according to OSHA the "equivalent noise exposure factor":

A. exceeds unity, therefore the noise exposure is within permissible levels

B. exceeds unity, therefore the noise exposure is not within permissible levels

C. Does not exceed unity, therefore the noise exposure is within permissible limits

D. does not exceed unity, therefore the noise exposure is not within permissible limits.

7. Exposure to impact or impulsive noise should not exceed _____ dB peak sound pressure.

A. 120   B. 130   C. 140   D. 15

8. Construction areas, aisles, stairs and ramps and storage areas for workers shall be lighted _____.

A. with natural illumination only

B. only if hazardous conditions

C. only if the job superintendent deems it necessary.

D. with natural or artificial illumination

9. According to OSHA, the minimum illumination of indoor corridors during construction is _____ foot candles.

A. 3   B. 5   C. 10   D. 30

10. Regarding personal protection life saving equipment, OD refers to_____.

A. over design   B. outside perimeter

C. optical density   D. operating difficulty

.

11. According to OSHA, life lines used for employee safeguarding shall have a minimum breaking strength of _____ pounds.

A. 500 pounds   B.4000   C.3500   D.5400

12. The maximum distance a man wearing a safety belt may drop or work is:

A. 3 feet   B. 6 feet   C. 12 feet   D. 15 feet

13. When working with scaffolds over water what precaution is required?

A. ever worker must wear safety shoes
B. all personnel should be instructed in life saving
C. all personnel should be wearing a life jacket or floatation, vest
D. scaffolds should not be build over water without safety nets

According to OSHA, a fire extinguisher rated not less than 2A shall be provided for each (maximum) of the protected building area.

A. 1500 sq. ft.   B. 2000 sq. ft.   C. 2500 sq. ft.   D. 3000 s

A fire breaks out in a main electrical junction box at a construction site, an electrician is lose by and asks you to get a fire extinguisher. According to OSHA, which of the following extinguishers should you bring back?

A. soda acid   B. foam
C. stored pressure (water type)   D. CO_2

16. A class A fire consists of burning_____ .

A. wood   B. oil
C. electrical equipment   D. metals

17. According to OSHA, material shall not be stored within _____ inches from a fire door:

A. 24 inches   B. 30 inches   C. 36 inches   D. 48 inches

18. According to OSHA, no more than _____ gallons of flammable or combustible liquids shall be stored in a room outside of an approved storage cabinet.

A. 10 gallons   B. 15 gallons   C. 20 gallons   D. 25 gallons

19. According to OSHA, a sign lettered in legible red letters, not less than 6 inches high on a white field is used only as a/an_____ sign.

A. danger   B. exit   C. caution   D. safety instructional

20. Material stored inside building under construction shall not be placed within _____ of any hoistway opening or inside floor openings.

A. 4'   B. 5'   C. 6'   D. 10'

21. Wire rope shall not be used if in any strength of 8 diameters the total number of visible broken wires exceed _____ % of the total number of wires.

A. 5   B. 10   C. 15   D. 20

22. According to OSHA, scaffolds and their components shall be capable of supporting without failure at least _____ times their maximum intended load.

A. 2   B. 3   C. 4   D. 5

23. Scaffold planks shall extend over end supports not less _____ inches and not more than _____ inches.

A. 6---12   B. 8---12   C. 9---12   D. 10---16

24. A standard toe board shall be a minimum of_____ inches high.

A. 3 inches   B. 3- 1/2 inches   C. 4 inches   D. 4- 1/2 inches

25. According to OSHA, the maximum permissible span for 2 x 10 inch planks used on scaffolding with a working load of 75 psf is_____feet. Assume full thickness, undressed lumber is used.

A. 10   B. 8   C. 6   D. 4

26. A gap or void 2 inches or more in its least dimension in a floor, roof, or other walking/working surface is a _____ .

A. toe hole   B. floor hole   C. breech   D. opening

27. According to OSHA, every open sided floor or platform (other than scaffolding) _____ feet or more above adjacent floor or ground level shall be guarded by a standard railing, or the equivalent, on all open sides, except where there is entrance to a ramp, stairway or fixed ladder.

A. 6 feet   B. 8 feet   C. 10 feet   D. 12 feet

28. The vertical height of a guard rail shall be:

A. 30 inches   B. 36 inches   C. 42 inches   D. 48 inches

29. Where electrical transmission lines are energized and rated at least 50 KV or less, a clearance of _____ feet minimum must be maintained by the crane and load.

A. 5 feet   B. 8 feet   C. 10 feet   D. 12 feet

30. According to OSHA safety and health regulation for construction, the minimum diameter wire ropes used in personnel hoists shall be _____ inch.

A. ½   B. 5/8   C. ¾   D. 7/8

31. When employees are required to be in trenches _____ feet or more in depth, ladders shall be provided for exit, and such ladders shall require not more than _____ feet of lateral travel.

A. 4 feet-30 feet   B. 5 feet- 30 feet
C. 4 feet-25 feet   D. 5 feet-25 feet

32. According to OSHA, when materials are dropped more than _____ feet outside the exterior walls of a building an enclosed chute must be utilized:

A. 10 feet   B. 15 feet   C. 20 feet   D. 25 feet

33. An electric power circular saw according to OSHA must be:

A. equipped with a constant pressure on switch
B. equipped with a momentary on/off switch that may have a lock on control
C. equipped with a positive on/off control,
D. none of the above

34. For general cleaning operations air pressure must be reduced to less than _____ psi.

A. 15   B. 20   C. 15   D. 30

35. Portable electrical tools do not have to be grounded if_____ .

A. they operate at less than 50 volts
B. equipped with a momentary on/off switch that may have lock on control
C. equipped with a positive on/off control
D. none of the above

36. Referring to power actuated tools, fasteners can be driven into _____.

A. face brick   B. surface hardened steel
C. cast iron   D. none of the above

37. According to OSHA, oxygen cylinders, regulators, and hoses shall be:

A. stored only in approved containers
B. prohibited in areas where fuel gasses other than acetylene are used
    unpainted
    kept free of all oil or grease

38. Class II hazardous locations are those with a presence of:

A. combustible dust   B. ignitable fibers
C. flammable liquids   D. explosives

39. When employees are required to be in trenches of _____ or more, an adequate means of exit such as a ladder or steps shall be provided.

A. 3 feet   B. 4 feet   C. 5 feet   D. 6 feet

40. In excavations where employees must enter, excavated or other materials may be stored:

A. two feet from the edge of the excavation
B. one foot from the edge of the excavation if properly retained
C. one foot from the edge of the excavation
D. A or B

41. The greatest angle above the horizontal plane for Type A soil is _____ degrees.

A. 34 degrees   B. 45 degrees   C. 53 degrees   D. 90 degrees

42. Sloping or benching for excavation than _____ feet deep shall be designed by a registered professional engineer.

A. 10   B. 15   C. 20   D. 25

43. OSHA requires that for skeleton steel construction no more than _____ feet or _____ floors of unfurnished bolting or welding exist:

A. 20 and 2   B. 24 and 2   C. 30 and 3   D. 48 and 4

44. The term "ROPS" means:

A. regional operating standards
B. required operating steps
C. roll over protective structures
D. none of the above

45. According to OSHA, temporary stairs shall have a landing not less than 30" in the direction of travel at every _____ (maximum) of vertical rise.

A. 8'   B. 10'   C. 12'   D. 16'

46. Temporary stairs shall be installed at angles to the horizontal of between _____ and _____ degrees.

A. 20 and 40   B. 20 and 50   C. 20 and 30   D. 30 and 50

47. According to OSHA, stairway railings shall be of such construction, to be capable of withstanding a minimum load of _____ pounds applied in any direction at any point the top rail.

A. 100   B. 150   C. 200   D. 250

48. Rungs, cleats and steps of portable ladders (except for special applications such as step-stools) shall be spaced not less than _____ inches, nor more than _____ inches.

A.8-11   B.8-14   C. 10-14   D. 12-16

49. The minimum clear distance between the side rails of all portable ladders shall not be less than _____ inches.

A. 11 ½   B. 12   C. 13   D. 14

50. A 27 foot ladder that extends the required distance above the landing should have a horizontal distance from the top support to the foot of the ladder of _____ feet.

A. 4   B. 5   C. 6   D. 8

What is the maximum base dimension for a 24 foot long cleat ladder with a top side rail spacing of 20 inches? Assume the side rail flare from top to bottom by not more than ¼ inch per each 2 feet of length.

A. 20"   B. 21"   C. 22"   D. 23"

The Code of Federal Regulations, 1926.1060, requires an employer to provide a training program for each employee:

A. using ladders and stairways
B. working with toxic substances
C. working in excavations
D. using scaffolding

53. Safety nets, where required, shall be provided when workplaces are more than <u>feet above </u>the ground or water surface.

A. 100
B. 75
C. 50
D. 25

OSHA Answer Sheet
PARAGRAPH 1926

1. D 32(n)
2. A Tb D-1
3. B 50(d)(2)
4. A 51(a)(2)&(5)
5. D Tb D-1
6. C 52 Tb
7. C 540
8. D 564
9. B 56 Tb D-3
10. C 102(b)(24
11. D 104(b)
12. B 104(d)
13. C 106(a)
14. D 150(c)
15. D Tb F-1
16. A Tb F-1
17. C 151(d)(7)
18. D 152(b)(2)
19. B 200(d)
20. C 250(b)(1)
21. B 251(c)(4)(iv)
22. C 451(a)(1)
23. A 451(b)(4) & (5)
24. B 451(h)(4)ii
25. C Sub. L, App. A
26. B 500(b)
27. A 501(b)(2)ii

28. C 502(b
29. C 550(a)(
30. A 552(c)(14)1
31. C 651(9)(2)
32. C 252(a)
33. A 300(d)(3)
34. D 302(b)(4)
35. D 302(a)
36. D 302(e)(7)
37. D 350(i)
38. A 449
39. B 651(c)(2)
40. D 651(j) (2)
41. C Tb B-1.
42. C Tb B-1 note
43. D 750(a)(2)
44. C 1000
45. C 1052(a)(1)
46. D 1052(a)(2)
47. C 1052(c)(5)
48. C 1053(a)(3)
49. A 1053(a)(4)
50. C 1053(b)(1)
51. D
52. A 1926.1060 (a)
53. D 1926.105 (a)

1 Exam Prep
OSHA Federal Safety and Health Regulations
Questions and Answers

1. According to O.S.H.A. Safety and Health Regulations, the minimum distance between the side rails of all portable ladders shall not be less than _____ inches.

      A. 11-1/2 inches   C. 13 inches
      B. 12 inches   D. 14 inches

When employees are required to be in trenches exit, and such ladders shall require not more than

          4 feet - 30 feet
          5 feet - 30 feet
          4 feet - 25 feet
          5 feet - 25 feet

feet or more in depth, ladders shall be provided for feet of lateral travel.

3. The dimension in the direction of travel on intermediate floor landings for temporary stairs shall be no less than _____ inches.

      A. 40 inches   C. 36 inches
      B. 30 inches   D. 24 inches

4. The toe boards of scaffolds shall be a minimum of _____ inches in height.

      A. 3-1/2 inches   C. 6 inches
      B. 4 inches   D. 8 inches

5. A scaffold used only by painters should be designed for a working load of _____ pounds per square foot (psf), if considered light duty.

      A. 15 psf   C. 25 psf
      B. 20 psf   D. 50 psf

6. A scaffold designed for 75 pounds per square foot (psf) would be usable for:

      A. painters   C. carpenters
      B. stone masons   D. all of above

What is the maximum base dimension for a 24 foot long, single cleat ladder with a topside rail spacing of 20 inches? Assume the side rail flare from top to bottom by not more than 1/4 inch per each two feet of length.

      A. 20 inches   C. 22 inches
      B. 21 inches   D. 23 inches

8. A bricklayer's square scaffold shall not exceed _____ feet in height and _____ feet in width.

A. 4 and 5   C. 3 and 4
B. 5 and 4   D. 5 and 5

The Code of Federal Regulations, 1926.1060, requires an employer to provide a training program for each employee:

    using ladders and stairways
    working with toxic substances
    working in excavations
    using scaffolding

According to O.S.H.A. Safety and Health Regulations, the required tests shall be performed on all cord sets and receptacles, which are not part of the permanent wiring of the building, which are fixed and not exposed to damage, at intervals not exceeding _____months.

A. 2 months   C. 4 months
B. 3 months   D. 6 months

11. According to O.S.H.A. Safety and Health Regulations, a 27-foot ladder that extends the required distance above the landing should have a horizontal distance from the top support to the foot of the ladder of ____ feet.

A. 4 feet   C. 6 feet
B. 5 feet   D. 8 feet

12. Personnel hoistway doors or gates shall be at least _____ high.

A. 4'-6"   C. 8'-6"
B. 6'-6"   D. none of above

13. According to O.S.H.A. Safety and Health Regulations, the minimum illumination for indoor corridors during construction is _____ foot-candles.

A. 3   C. 10
B. 5   D. 30

14. Scaffolding guard rails shall be approximately _____high with supports not to exceed _____feet.

A. 36" and 6'
B. 42" and 6'
C. 48" and 6'
D. 42" and 8'

Scaffolding designed for stone masons must be "heavy duty", that is, designed for a working load of pounds per square food (psf).

A. 25 psf
B. 50 psf

C. 75 psf
D. 100 psf

16. A standard toe board shall be equivalent in strength to 1 inch by _____ inches high.

A. 3 inches
B. 3-1/2 inches

C. 4 inches
D. 4-1/2 inches

One 40-gallon open drum of water with 2 fire pails may be substituted for fire extinguishers having a 2A rating.

A. true

B. false

The recommended horizontal distance from the top support to the front of a portable ladder with a working length of 24 feet is:

A. 2 feet
B. 3 feet

C. 4 feet
D. 6 feet

19. Rungs, cleats and steps of portable ladders (except for special applications such as step-stools) shall be spaced not less than _____ inches, nor more than _____.

A. 8 - 11
B. 9 - 14

C. 10 - 14
D. 12 - 16

20. Wire rope shall not be used for material handling if any length of _____ the total number of visible broken wires exceeds 10% of the total number of wires:

A. 12 inches
B. 18 inches

C. one lag
D. 8 diameters

21. According to O.S.H.A. Safety and Health Regulations, the minimum illumination of an indoor warehouse is _____ floor candles:

A. 3
B. 5

C. 10
D. 12

All new safety nets shall meet accepted performance standards as follows:

17,500 foot pounds minimum impact resistance
24,000 foot pounds minimum impact resistance
withstand five 200 pound sacks dropped simultaneously from a height of 25 feet
10,000 pound rope tensile strength

On stairways more than 44 inches wide, but less than 88 inches wide, hand rails are required:

      only on the open sides
      if both sides are enclosed, only one hand rail
      on each side
      on each side, and one in the center

If the personnel hoist wire rope speed is 300 feet per minute, the minimum rope safety factor must be:

A. 9.20	C. 9.75
B. 9.50	D. 10.00

25. The use of non-self supporting ladders shall be at such an angle that the horizontal distance from the top support to the foot of the ladder is approximately _____ of the working length of the ladder.

A. one half	C. three quarters
B. one quarter	D. seven eighths

26. Temporary stairs shall be installed at angles to the horizontal of between and _____ degrees.

A. 20 and 40	C. 20 and 30
B. 20 and 50	D. 30 and 50

Wherever there is a danger of falling through a skylight hole

      it must be guarded by a fixed standard railing
      it must be covered to sustain an 800 pound load
      it must be covered to sustain a 200 pound person
      either A or C is correct

Class II hazardous locations are those with a presence of:

A. combustible dust	C. flammable liquids
B. ignitable fibers	D. explosives

29. Open yard storage of combustible materials limits the height of the piles to _____ feet.

A. 12 feet	C. 16 feet
B. 14 feet	D. 20 feet

In excavations where employees must enter, excavated or other materials may be stored:

      two feet from the edge of the excavation
      one foot from the edge of the excavation if properly retained
      one foot from the edge of the excavation
      A or B

31. O.S.H.A. Safety and Health Regulations requires that for skeleton steel construction no more than _____ feet or _____ floors of unfinished bolting or welding exist:

    A. 20 and 2
    B. 24 and 2
    C. 30 and 3
    D. 48 and 4

The term "ROPS" means:

    Regional Operating Standards
    Required Operating Steps
    Roll over Protective Structures
    None of the above

33. The greatest angle above the horizontal plan for Type A soil is _____ degrees.

    A. 34°   C. 53°
    B. 45°   D. 90°

34. The maximum allowable slope for Type A soil for a simple slope in an excavation of 20 feet or less in depth is _____ horizontal to _____ vertical.

    A. 1 to 1   C. 1/2 to 1
    B. 2 to 1   D. 3/4 to 1

According to O.S.H.A. Safety and Health Regulations, the recommended slope for sides of excavations for average soil (Type B) is:

    A. 45°   C. 60°
    B. 55°   D. 70°

When employees are required to be in trenches of or more, an adequate means of exit such as a ladder or steps shall be provided.

    A. 3 feet
    B. 4 feet
C. 5 feet
D. 6 feet

Openings are defined as a gap or void:

    12 inches or less in its least dimension
    30" or more high and 18" or more wide
    less than 12 inches but more than 1 inch in its least dimension
    12 inches or more in its greatest dimension

38. The vertical height of a guard rail shall be:

      A. 30 inches
      B. 36 inches
C 42 inches
D. 48 inches

The use of a spiral stair for construction purposes shall be:

      not permitted
      permitted if permanent part of structure
      normally prohibited
      at least 7 feet in diameter

According to O.S.H.A. Safety and Health Regulations, the side rails of portable ladders shall extend a minimum _____ of above the landing.

A. 22 inches	C. 30 inches
B. 24 inches	D. 36 inches

41. One toilet shall be provided at the construction job site for a maximum of _____ employees.

A. 5 employees	C. 15 employees
B. 10 employees	D. 20 employees

42. A class C fire is a type fire:

      A. combustible metal
      B. flammable liquid
C. trash
D. electrical

The maximum allowable slope for excavations less than 20 feet deep for compacted sharp sand (Type C soil) is:

A. 90°	C. 45°
B. 63°	D. 34°

According to O.S.H.A. Safety and Health Regulations, when materials are dropped more than feet outside the exterior walls of a building an enclosed chute must be utilized:

      A. 10 feet
      B. 15 feet
C. 20 feet
D. 25 feet

According to O.S.H.A. Safety and Health Regulations, material shall not be stored indoors within inches from a fire door:

      A. 24 inches
      B. 30 inches
C. 36 inches
D. 48 inches

46. According to O.S.H.A. Safety and Health Regulations, scaffold planking that is nominal 2" thick can be used for a _____ psf workload at a maximum span of _____ feet.

A. 25 and 10   C. 75 and 6
B. 50 and 8   D. 25 and 8

O.S.H.A. Safety and Health Regulations requires a safety factor based on load and speed be used in hoist cables. The safety factor for a cable with a speed of 200 feet per minute is:

A. 7.00   C. 7.65
B. 6.65   D. 8.60

48. According to O.S.H.A. Safety and Health Regulations, life lines used for employee safeguarding shall have a minimum breaking strength of _____ pounds.

A. 500 pounds   C. 3,500 pounds
B. 1,000 pounds   D. 5,400 pounds

According to O.S.H.A. Safety and Health Regulations, the proper maintenance for a carbon dioxide type fire extinguisher is to:

      discharge annually and recharge
      check pressure gauge monthly
      check pressure gauge annually
      weigh semi-annually

50. According to O.S.H.A. Safety and Health Regulations, no more than _____ gallons of flammable or combustible liquids shall be stored in a room outside of an approved storage cabinet.

A. 10 gallons   C. 20 gallons
B. 15 gallons   D. 25 gallons

51. According to O.S.H.A. Safety and Health Regulations, exposure to impulsive or impact noise shall not exceed _____ dBA peak sound pressure level.

A. 110 dBA   C. 120 dBA
B. 115 dBA   D. 140 dBA

52. Simple slope - short-term excavations with a maximum depth of 12 feet can be sloped to a maximum of _____ horizontal to _____ vertical for Type A soil.

A. 1 to 1   C. 3/4 to 1
B. 2 to 1   D. 1/2 to 1

O.S.H.A. Safety and Health Regulations state that shore or leant-to scaffolding:

> is restricted to structures having 4 or less stories
> is restricted to structures having 3 or less stories
> has to be made to hold a dead weight load of 20 psi
> is prohibited

Wire, synthetic or fiber rope used for scaffold suspension shall be capable of supporting at least _____ times the rated load.

> A. 6 times
> B. 7 times

C. 8 times

D. 9 times

According to O.S.H.A. Safety and Health Regulations, the proper maintenance for a multi-purpose ABC dry chemical stored pressure fire extinguisher is to:

> check pressure gauge monthly
> discharge annually and recharge
> weigh semi-annually
> check pressure gauge and condition of dry chemical annually

According to O.S.H.A. Safety and Health Regulations, metal tubular frame scaffolds, including accessories such as braces, brackets, trusses, screws legs, ladders, etc. shall be designed, constructed and erected to safely support _____ times the maximum load.

A. 1-1/2 times	C. 3 times
B. 2 times	D. 4 times

According to O.S.H.A. Safety and Health Regulations, the maximum span of 2" x 10" undressed lumber on a scaffold when loaded with 50 PSI is:

A. 5 feet	C. 7 feet
B. 6 feet	D. 8 feet

58. On construction sites, a fire extinguisher rated not less than 2A shall be provided for each _____ square feet of the protected building area, or major fraction thereof.

A. 1,000 SF	C. 3,000 SF
B. 2,000 SF	D. 4,000 SF

A stairway abutts a building on one side, has the opposite side open has a total of 14 risers per flight, and is _____ inches wide. According to O.S.H.A. Safety and Health Regulations, the stairway:

> does not require any railings or handrails
> must be equipped with at least one stair railing on the open side
> must be rebuilt to contain not more than 10 risers per flight and must be equipped with one stair railing on the open side
> must be equipped with one handrail on the enclosed side and one stair railing on the open side

60. According to O.S.H.A. Safety and Health Regulations, every open sided floor or platform (other than scaffolding) feet or more above adjacent floor or ground level shall be guarded by a standard railing, or the equivalent, on all open sides, except where there is entrance to a ramp, stairway or fixed ladder.

    A. 6 feet
    B. 8 feet

C. 10 feet
D. 12 feet

61. Where electrical transmission lines are energized and rated at least 50 kW or less, a clearance of _____ feet minimum must be maintained by the crane and load.

    A. 5 feet   C. 10 feet
    B. 8 feet   D. 12 feet

62. The maximum distance a man wearing a safety belt may drop or work is:
    A. 3 feet
    B. 6 feet
C. 12 feet
D. 15 feet

63. The maximum allowable height of a horse scaffold of two tiers is:
    A. 4 feet
    B. 8 feet
C. 12 feet
D. 10 feet

    According to O.S.H.A. Safety and Health Regulations, a carpenters bracket scaffold:
        brackets shall be spaced a maximum of 8 feet
        may be used if bolted to the wall
        may be used if hooked over the top of a wall
        all of the above
    When a material hoist tower is not enclosed:
        the hoist platform shall be caged on all sides
        shall have 1/2 inch mesh number 16 U.S. gage wire covering
        shall have a five foot enclosure at ground level
        all of the above

66. Employees cannot be subjected to noise levels higher than _____ decibels for more than four hours per day according to O.S.H.A. Safety and Health Regulations.

    A. 95 dB   B. 10dB
    C. 102 dB   D. 105dB

67. The range of working loads from light to heavy-duty independent pole scaffolds is _____ pounds per square foot (PSF).

    A. 20 - 75 PSF   C. 25 - 75 PSF
    B. 25 - 70 PSF   D. 25 - 50 PSF

According to O.S.H.A. Safety and Health Regulations, which of the following statements is NOT true:

> a trench sloped at the angle of repose need to be braced
> when bracing and shoring is required, it shall be carried along with the excavation
> trenches more than four feet in depth shall have ladders placed at intervals for ready entrance and exit
> trenches more than four feet in depth shall be shored and braced unless in solid rock

69. According to O.S.H.A. Safety and Health Regulations, no more than _____ employees shall occupy and given 8 feet of a bracket scaffold.

A. 1 employee
B. 2 employees
C. 3 employees
D. 4 employees

The minimum clearance between an operating crane and energized and unprotected electrical distribution lines (rated at 35 kV), shall be:

A. 10 feet
B. 14 feet
C. 16 feet
D. 20 feet

71. Given the following:
1-1/2 hours noise exposure at 90 dBA
½ hour noise exposure at 100 dBA
½ hour noise exposure at 105 dBA

If your employees are exposed to all of the above noise levels each workday, then according to O.S.H.A. Safety and Health Regulations, the "Equivalent Noise Exposure Factor":

A. exceeds unity, therefore the noise exposure is within permissible levels
B. exceeds unity, therefore the noise exposure is not within permissible levels
C. does not exceed unity, therefore the noise exposure is within permissible limits
D. does not exceed unity, therefore the noise exposure is not within permissible limits

A fire breaks out in a main electrical junction box at a construction site, an electrician is close by and asks you to get a fire extinguisher. According to O.S.H.A. Safety and Health Regulations, which of the following extinguisher should you bring back:

A. soda acid
B. foam
C. stored pressure (water type)
D. CO_2

According to O.S.H.A. Safety and Health Regulations, oxygen cylinders, regulators and hoses shall be:

> stored only in approved containers
> prohibited in areas where fuel gasses other than acetylene are used
> unpainted
> kept free of all oil or grease

A female employee complains that there are not separate toilets for the 20 women working on the site.

She further states that all 160 employees use the same toilet. She said that the contractor is not complying with O.S.H.A. According to O.S.H.A. Safety and Health Standards, the employee _____.

> A. does not have a valid complaint since O.S.H.A. has no specific instructions as to male and female toilets. The project is only required to have four toilets and four urinals
> B. does not have a valid complaint since O.S.H.A. has no specific instructions as to male and female toilets. The project is only required to have five toilets and five urinals
> C. has a valid complaint since O.S.H.A. specifies that five toilets and five urinals for men and a separate toilet for women are required on a project of that size
> D. has a valid complaint since O.S.H.A. specifies five toilets and four urinals for men and a separate toilet for women are required on a project of that size.

Employees shall not be support to noise levels exceeding _____ for more than four hours a day.

> 95 dB
> 10 dB
> 102 dB
> 105 dB

The minimum clear distance between side rails for all portable ladders shall be _____ inches.

> 11-½
> 12
> 13
> 14

Portable electric lightning used in wet and /or other conductive locations shall be operated at _____ or less.

> 12 volts
> 32 volts
> 110 volts
> 220 volts

_____ shall not be used if the rope shows other signs of excessive wear, corrosion, or defect.

Alloy steel chains
Synthetic fiber rope
Natural rope
Wire rope

_____ shall be spaced not less than 10 inches apart, nor more than 14 inches apart.

Fixed ladders
Rungs
Steps of portable ladders
All of the above

One 55-gallon open drum of water with two fire pails may be substituted for a fire extinguisher having a 2A rating.

True
False

See Answer Key below

.

1 Exam Prep
OSHA Federal Safety and Health Regulations
Answers – Part 1926

1. A .1053(a)(4)(ii)
2. C .651(c)(2)
3. B .1052(a)(1)
4. A .502(j)(3)
5. C Subpart L, Appendix A
6. D Subpart L, Appendix A
7. D
8. D Subpart L, Appendix A
9. C 1926.651 (b) (1)
10. D .404(b)(1)(iii)(E)(4)
11. C .1053(b)(5)(L)
12. B .552(c)(4)
13. B .56, Table D-3
14. D Subpart L, Appendix A
15. C .451(g)(4)(ii)
16. C Subpart L, Appendix A
17. B .150(c)(1)(ii)
18. D .1053(b)(5)(1)
19. C .1053(a)(3)(L)
20. D .251(c)(4)(iv)
21. B .56, Table D-3
22. A .105(d)
23. C .1052(c)(1)(ii)
24. A .552(c)(14)(iii)
25. B .1053(b)(5)(i)
26. D .1052(a)(2)
27. D .501(b)(4) & .502(b)(4)
28. A .449
29. D .151(c) & .250(b)(8)(iv)
30. D .651(j)(2)
31. D .754(b)(2)
32. C .1000
33. C Subpart P, Appendix B, Table B-1
34. D Subpart P, Appendix B, Table B-1
35. A Subpart P, Appendix B, Table B-1
36. B .651(c)(2)
37. B .500(b)
38. C .502(b)(1)
39. B .1051(a)(1)
40. D .1053(b)(1)

41. D .51, Table D- 1
42. D Subpart F, Table F-1
43. D Subpart P, Appendix B, Table B-1
44. C .252(a)
45. C .151(d)(7)
46. D Subpart L, Appendix A
47. D .552(c)(14)(iii)
48. D .104(d)
49. D Subpart F, Table F-1
50. D .152(d)
51. D .52(e)
52. D Subpart P.
53. D .451(0(2)
54. A .451(a)(4)
55. D Subpart F, Table F-1
56. D .451(a)
57. D Subpart L, Appendix A
58. C .150(c)
59. D .1052(c)
60. A .501(b)(1)
61. C .550(a)(15)(i)
62. B .104(d)
63. D .452(f)
64. D Subpart L, Appendix A, Paragraph (g)
65. A .552(b)(5)(ii)
66. A .52, Table D-2
67. C Subpart L, Appendix A
68. D Subpart P
69. B Subpart L, Appendix A, Paragraph (g)
70. A .550(a)(15)(i)
71. C .52 (d)(2)(iii)
72. D Subpart F, Table F-1
73. D .350(i)
74. A .51(c)
75. A
76. A
77. A
78. D
79. D
80. A

Florida Building Code-Building, 2017
Questions and Answers

Garages designed and built to accommodate heavy vehicles shall be able to handle weights that exceed _____.

    6,000 pounds
    8,000 pounds
    10,000 pounds
    12,000 pounds

What is the net cross-sectional area of a rectangular chimney flue that is 12" x 16"?

    A. 101"
       102"
    C. 127"
    D. 131"

Non-bearing walls and partitions in conventional light-frame construction shall have a MAXIMUM stud spacing of _____.

    A. 16" o.c.
    B. 20" o.c.
    C. 24" o.c.
    D. 28" o.c.

What is the MINIMUM required width of a pedestrian walkway in front of a construction or demolition site?

    4 feet
    5 feet
    6 feet
    7 feet

What is the MINIMUM height of a protective barrier or fence enclosing a residential swimming pool?

    42"
    48"
    54"
    60"

When excavating a hole within 5 feet of the street lot line, the hole shall have a protective barrier with a MINIMUM height of_____

     5 feet.
     6 feet.
     7 feet.
     8 feet.

In a building that only has one elevator, how long before the elevator shall automatically transfer to standby power after the failure of the normal power supply?

     Within 15 seconds
     Within 30 seconds
     Within 45 seconds
     Within 60 seconds

8. Air supported and air inflated structures larger than 1,500 square feet shall have an auxiliary inflation system that is powered by a standby power system. What is the MINIMUM amount of time the standby power system must operate independently?

     A. 1 hour
     B. 2 hours
     C. 3 hours
     D. 4 hours

Handrails and guards shall be designed to resist a linear load. What is the load amount?

     50 linear pounds per foot
     60 linear pounds per foot
     70 linear pounds per foot
     80 linear pounds per foot

When vinyl siding is installed horizontally, what is the MAXIMUM fastener spacing?

     A. 14"
     B. 16"
     C. 18"
     D. 20"

What is the MINIMUM thickness of exterior poured concrete basement and foundation walls with a MAXIMUM height of 8 feet and assigned to Seismic Design Category D or E?

     A. 6.0"
     B. 6.5"
     7.0"
     7.5"

Platform lifts used as a component of an accessible route for wheelchairs shall comply with what ICC Standard?

A117.1
A118.1
A136.1
A137.1

Each dwelling unit shall have at least one room that has a MINIMUM square footage of_____

100 sq. feet.
120 sq. feet.
140 sq. feet.
160 sq. feet.

When constructing an artificial barricade in the form of a mound or revetment, what is the MINIMUM required thickness?

3 feet
4 feet
5 feet
6 feet

When installing a foundation drain, the drain pipe shall be placed around the exterior of the perimeter and extend what MINIMUM distance beyond the edge of the foundation?

A. 10"
B. 12"
C. 14"
D. 16"

What is the MAXIMUM allowed travel distance from a tenant space on an accessible route to a drinking fountain in a covered mall building?

300 feet
400 feet
500 feet
600 feet

What is the MINIMUM design live load for the entire length of a pedestrian covered walkway?

120 psf
130 psf
140 psf
150 psf

In a building that contains commercial cooking equipment, what is the MAXIMUM distance that a portable fire extinguisher can be installed from the cooking equipment?

    10 feet
    20 feet
    30 feet
    40 feet

A residential aircraft hanger building shall have a MAXIMUM height of 20 feet with a MAXIMUM allowed square footage of

    2,000 sq. ft.
    2,500 sq. ft.
    3,000 sq. ft.
    3,500 sq. ft.

20. What is the MAXIMUM distance between fasteners on 1/2" gypsum board used for a horizontal diaphragm ceiling?

    A. 7" on center
    B. 8" on center
    C. 9" on center
    D. 10" on center

In a building that requires a fire command center, the walls shall be of 1-hour fire barrier construction with a MINIMUM dimension of 10 feet and a MINIMUM square footage of_____

    175 with a minimum dimension of 10 feet.
    200 with a minimum dimension of 10 feet.
    225 with a minimum dimension of 10 feet.
    250 with a minimum dimension of 10 feet.

What is the MINIMUM size wood column used to support roof and ceiling loads only?

    A. 6" x 8"
    B. 6" x 10"
    C. 8" x 8"
    D. 8" x 10"

Which of the two following types of mortar which conform to ASTM C270 can be used on glass unit masonry construction?

    O and S
    N and O
    S and N
    M and N

What MAXIMUM amount of time delay is allowed before a smoke actuated door must close when activated by smoke detectors?

    10 seconds
    15 seconds
    20 seconds
    25 seconds

In what type of construction are timber footings allowed to be used?

    Type I
    Type II
    Type III
    Type V

A commercial cooking fire extinguishing system shall have a manual actuation switch located what

    A. 30"
    B. 36"
    C. 42"
    48"

What is the MINIMUM thickness required for a lightweight, cast-in-place concrete wall to achieve a 1.5 hour-fire-resistance rating?

    2.5"
    B. 3.1"
    C. 3.6"
    D. 4.4"

What is the MINIMUM compressive strength of concrete after 28 days?

    2,800 psi
    3,000 psi
    3,200 psi
    3,400 psi

What is the MINIMUM size covered mall building that is required to have a standby power system?

    Greater than 40,000 sq. feet
    Greater than 50,000 sq. feet
    Greater than 60,000 sq. feet
    Greater than 70,000 sq. feet

What is the MAXIMUM number of elevator cars that can be located in one hoist way enclosure?

    1 car
    2 cars
    3 cars
    4 cars

Unless otherwise indicated, what size area shall a concentrated load be considered uniformly distributed over?

   2 feet by 2 feet
   2-1/2 feet by 2-1/2 feet
   3 feet by 3 feet
   3-1/2 feet by 3-1/2 feet

What distance above the public right-of-way can an encroachment be mounted and not be limited in size?
   12 feet
   13 feet
   14 feet
   15 feet

In a building that is classified as an F-1 occupancy, how many water closets are required?

   1 per 15 people
   1 per 50 people
   1 per 100 people
   1 per 500 people

Family or assisted-use toilet and bathing rooms count toward the required fixtures in an assembly occupancy. In what other type of occupancy do these facilities count toward fixture totals?

   Business
   Educational
   Mercantile
   Factory

What is the MINIMUM ceiling height is required for a means of egress?

   A. 7' 0" feet
   B. 7' 6" feet
   C. 8' 0" feet
   D. 8' 6" feet

What MINIMUM dimension column would be required to achieve a 4 hour fire-resistance rating using carbonate concrete?

   A. 9"
      10"
      11"
      12"

What is the MAXIMUM exit access travel distance in a building that is an S-1 occupancy that is with automatic sprinkler system?

   200 feet
   250 feet
   300 feet
   400 feet

What is the MAXIMUM height of a penthouse built on a building (other than a Type I building) to contain air conditioning equipment and piping?

    12 feet
    15 feet
    18 feet
    21 feet

What is the MINIMUM distance above the plane of a roof that sloped glazing or skylights can be mounted on a curb?

    A. 2"
    B. 4"
    C. 6"
    D. 8"

When a preconstruction load test is conducted, what is the required amount of time the test shall be left in place?

    12 hours
    16 hours
    24 hours
    30 hours

41. What size and type of nails should be used to secure 2" planks?

    A. 8d common
    B. 10d common
    C. 16d common
    D. 20d common

What is the MAXIMUM size reinforcement bar that can be used with shotcrete?

    No. 5
    No. 6
    No. 7
    No. 8

What is the MINIMUM number of fasteners that shall be used per wood shake?

    1 fastener
    2 fasteners
    3 fasteners
    4 fasteners

What is the MAXIMUM area of a Group U building that is a Type IIA construction?

    8,500 sq. feet
    14,000 sq. feet
    19,000 sq. feet
    35,500 sq. feet

What MAXIMUM thickness insulating boards can be installed under approved finish flooring when installed using permitted conditions?

    A. 3/8"
    B. 1/2"
    C. 5/8"
    5. 3/4"

Footings used for a masonry fireplace shall be constructed of cement or solid masonry with a MINIMUM thickness of

    A. 8"
    B. 10"
    C. 12"
    D. 14"

What is the MAXIMUM size of a tire warehouse before an automatic sprinkler system throughout the building is required?

    14,000 cubic feet
    16,000 cubic feet
    18,000 cubic feet
    20,000 cubic fee

What is the MINIMUM nominal thickness in at least one direction for wood framing supporting gypsum board or lath?

    A. 1"
    B. 2"
    C. 3"
    D. 4"

49. What is the MINIMUM width for an exit passageway or corridor from a mall?

    A. 60"
    B. 66"
    C. 72"
    D. 78"

Foam plastic spray insulation applied to a sill plate and header in a Type V construction shall have a MAXIMUM thickness of

    A. 2.75".
    B. 3.00".
    C. 3.25".
    D. 3.50".

51. What MINIMUM size sawn or glued-laminated wood beams and girders shall be used for floor framing?

    A. 6" x 10"
    B. 8" x 10"
    C. 6" x 12"
    D. 8" x 12"

When a pedestrian barrier is required at a construction site, what is the MINIMUM height that the barrier shall be built extending the entire length of the site?

    6 feet
    8 feet
    10 feet
    12 feet

Buildings that are over 4 stories in height shall have at least one elevator capable of carrying an ambulance stretcher in the horizontal position. What MINIMUM length will the elevator have to be to accommodate the stretcher?

    76"
    78"
    80"
    82"

A _____ Group occupancy is the general classification for miscellaneous and utility structures.

    A
    M
    S
    U

Interior spaces intended for human occupancy shall have a heating system capable of maintaining what level of temperature measured 3 feet off the floor?

    68°F
    69°F
    70°F
    71°F

A bowling alley shall be designed for a MINIMUM uniformly distributed live floor load of_____

   75 psf.
   100 psf.
   125 psf.
   150 psf.

What is the MINIMUM clear width of each door opening in a commercial building?

   A. 31"
   B. 32"
   C. 33"
   D. 34"

The MAXIMUM allowable number of stories in height for a Group H-4 occupancy building not equipped throughout with an automatic sprinkler system and built with Type IIB construction is _____ stories.

   2
   3
   4
   5

What is the MAXIMUM allowed travel distance to toilet facilities in an office building for employees and the public?

   200 feet
   300 feet
   400 feet
   500 feet

What is the MINIMUM size access opening to a building attic?

   A. 20" x 30"
   B. 24" x 30"
   C. 30" x 30"
   D. 30" x 36"

What MINIMUM height above a public right-of-way must the lowest part of an awning, including the valance, maintain?

   A. 6' 6"
   B. 7' 0"
   C. 7' 6"
   D. 8' 0"

A temporary structure is required to have a permit when it is designed to hold at least 10 occupants and have a square footage in excess of

    100 sq. feet.
    120 sq. feet.
    140 sq. feet.
    160 sq. feet.

An incinerator room is classified as an incidental accessory occupancy. What is the required separation and/or protection?

    1 hour separation or a fire extinguishing system
    1 hour separation and an automatic sprinkler system
    2 hour separation and a fire extinguishing system
    2 hour separation and an automatic sprinkler system

What two types of mortar are approved for laying masonry unit footings?

    Type O or S
    Type N or O
    Type M or N
    Type M or S

When cement exterior plaster is being applied to a building, the temperature must be above what temperature?

    40°F
    42°F
    44°F
    46°F

An automatic sprinkler system is required throughout the building in a Group E occupancy when the fire area exceeds_____

    A. 6,000 sq. feet.
    B. 8,000 sq. feet.
    C. 10,000 sq. feet.
    D. 12,000 sq. feet.

The bottom of a footing shall be located a minimum of _____ inches below the undisturbed ground surface.

    6
    12
    15
    18

Concrete used for building foundations included in Seismic Design Category A, B or C shall have what MINIMUM specified compressive strength?

      2,500 psi
      2,800 psi
      3,000 psi.
      3,200 psi.

What is the MAXIMUM height for an aircraft control tower built with Type IB construction?

      65 feet
      85 feet
      100 feet
      240 feet

A shaft enclosure shall have a minimum 2-hour fire-resistance rating where connecting a minimum of _____ stories.

      Two
      Three
      Four
      Six

What MINIMUM lap is required when installing horizontal fiber-cement siding?

      A. 1"
      1.25"
      1.50"
      1.75"

What is the MAXIMUM exit access travel distance on a pedestrian walkway that has both sides at least 50% open and has an automatic sprinkler system through the entire distance of the walkway installed?

      250 feet
      300 feet
      350 feet
      400 feet

Glazing in an individual window, either fixed or operable, shall be considered a hazardous location if the exposed area of an individual pane is more than

      7 square feet.
      8 square feet.
      9 square feet.
      10 square feet

Manual fire alarm boxes shall be located not more than 5 feet from entry to each exit with a MAXIMUM distance between additional manual fire alarm boxes of

    100 feet.
    200 feet.
    300 feet.
    400 feet.

What is the MINIMUM thickness of the concrete footings required for a masonry chimney?

A. 12"
B. 14"
C. 16"
D. 18"

The stability of interior finish products shall be applied or fastened in a manner to prevent the product from becoming detached when subjected to room temperatures of _____.

    200°F for a minimum of 30 minutes.
    225°F for a minimum of 30 minutes.
    250°F for a minimum of 45 minutes.
    250°F for a minimum of 60 minutes.

What MAXIMUM distance are steps allowed to project into the public right-of-way?

A. 8"
B. 10"
C. 12"
D. 14"

What shall be the MINIMUM fire-resistance rating for interior bearing walls in a Type IIA construction?

    0 hour
    1 hour
    2 hours
    3 hours

Walk-in coolers in un sprinkled buildings shall have a MAXIMUM foam plastic wall thickness of 4" and shall not exceed an aggregate floor area of_____

    250 sq. feet.
    300 sq. feet.
    350 sq. feet.
    400 sq. feet.

What is the MAXIMUM flame spread index allowed for fire-retardant-treated wood?

    10
    15
    20
    25

What is the MINIMUM separation between skylights when measured in a horizontal plane?

    4 feet
    5 feet
    6 feet
    7 feet

Open web steel joists must be manufactured to specifications from the Steel Joist Institute. Which of the following is NOT a specification from SJI?

    SJI K
    SJI M
    SJI LH/DLH
    SJI JG

What type of construction is classified as heavy timber?

    Type I
    Type II
    Type III
    Type IV

What is the MINIMUM width of a walkway for pedestrians passing a construction site?

    A. 42"
    B. 48"
    C. 54"
    D. 60"

Which of the following buildings would be classified as an A-2 occupancy?

    Theaters
    Arenas
    Libraries
    Restaurants

What is the MINIMUM fire barrier assembly resistance between fire areas for an S-2 occupancy group?

    1 hour
    2 hours
    3 hours
    4 hours

The aggregate area of a mezzanine within a room shall be not greater than _____ of the floor area of that room or space in which they are located.

        one-quarter
        one-third
        one-half
        three-quarters

What is the MAXIMUM listed flame spread index for wood that has been impregnated with fire retardant chemicals through the pressure process?

        10
        25
        50
        75

All of the following products can be stored in an S-2 occupancy EXCEPT

        frozen food.
        glass.
        furniture.
        mirrors.

What is the MINIMUM period of moist curing time required for the second coat of cement plaster?

        24 hours
        32 hours
        40 hours
        48 hours

What is the MINIMUM clear width of an escalator that provides service to a below-grade transportation station?

        A. 32"
        B. 34"
        C. 36"
        D. 38"

What is the MAXIMUM flame spread index for foam plastic insulation greater than 4 inches?

        25
        50
        75
        100

93. When fiber-cement siding is installed on a building with wood studs, the siding shall be fastened with corrosion-resistant round head smooth shank nails that will penetrate the studs a MINIMUM of_____

    A. 5/8".
    B. 3/4".
    C. 7/8".
    D. 1".

Interior wall and ceiling finishes are classified with ASTM E 84. What is the flame spread rating for a Class C finish?

    0-25
    26-75
    76-200
    201-300

What is the MINIMUM height of a parapet from the point it insects with the roof's surface to the top of the parapet?

    A. 24"
    B. 30"
    C. 36"
    4"

Beginning the construction of a new building requires an excavation be dug. The owners of the adjacent buildings must be notified of the upcoming excavation not less than

    4 days prior to the scheduled starting date.
    6 days prior to the scheduled starting date.
    8 days prior to the scheduled starting date.
    10 days prior to the scheduled starting date.

What MINIMUM amount of glazing is required to give a room natural light?

    6% of the floor area of the room served
    8% of the floor area of the room served
    10% of the floor area of the room served
    12% of the floor area of the room served

In order to avoid aerodynamic lift, concrete and clay roof tiles shall be single lapped interlocking with a MINIMUM head lap of not less than_____ inches.

    2
    3
    4
    5

Door handles, pulls, latches, locks and other operating devices shall be installed _____ inches minimum and _____ inches maximum above the finished floor.

    30 - 50
    32 - 50
    34 - 48
    36 - 48

Concrete or masonry walls below grade shall have waterproofing installed from the bottom of the wall to how far above the MAXIMUM height of the ground-water table?

    A. 6"
    B. 12"
    C. 18"
    D. 24"

101. What is stamped on construction documents after they have been reviewed by the building department?

    A. "Accepted for Code Compliance"
    B. "Reviewed for Code Compliance"
    C. "Approved for Code Compliance"
    D. "Processed for Code Compliance"

What is the MAXIMUM thickness of stone veneer that can be anchored directly to masonry, concrete or stud construction?

    8"
    10"
    12"
    14"

What is the MAXIMUM length of glass sections used in louvered windows or jalousies?

    A. 48"
    B. 52"
    56"
    60"

Which of the following hazard categories requires barricade construction for explosion control?

    Cryogenic flammables
    Organic peroxides
    Flammable liquids
    Pyrophoric gas

105. What is the MINIMUM nominal thickness of a chimney wall made with solid masonry units?

    A. 2"
    B. 3"
    C. 4"
    D. 5"

In what Residential Group R would a residential board and care/assisted living facility be categorized?

    R-1
    R-2
    R-3
    R-4

Several different types of glazing can be used in handrails and guards. What is the MINIMUM thickness of the glass (no matter what type of glass is used)?

    A. 1/8"
    B. 1/4"
    C. 3/8"
    D. 1/2"

The thickness of concrete floor slabs supported directly on the ground shall not be less than _____ inches.

    3
    3 ½
    4
    4 ½

Which of the following mechanical systems DOES require a permit?

    Replacement of a minor part
    Use of a portable cooling unit
    Use of a portable ventilation appliance
    Replacement of a complete boiler

What is the MINIMUM thickness of interior load-bearing walls made of adobe masonry for a one-story building?

    A. 8"
      10"
    C. 12"
    D. 14"

Micropiles shall have an outside diameter of _____ inches or less.

12
14
16
18

If there is no conflict in the code between a general requirement and a specific requirement, the _____ requirement shall apply.

General
Specific
Least restrictive
Most Restrictive

Used materials may be utilized under which of the following conditions?

They meet the requirements for new materials.
They are limited to 10 percent of the total materials.
Used materials may never be used in new construction.
A representative sampling is tested for compliance

114.. The building permit, or a copy of the permit, shall be kept _____ until completion of the project.

A. At the job site
B. By the permit applicant
C. By the contractor
D. By the design professional in responsible charge

Whose duty is it to notify the building official that the work is ready for inspection?

The permit holder
The owner
The contractor
The architect

One set of approved construction documents shall be retained by the building official for a period of not less than _____ days from date of completion of the permitted work.

30
90
120
180

The _____ is responsible for assuring that the work is accessible and exposed for inspection purposes.

    Owner
    Contractor
    Permit applicant
    Design professional

A stop work order shall be in writing and given to any of the following individuals except the _____.

    Owner of the property involved
    Owner's agent
    Permit holder
    Person doing the work

An institutional occupancy is typically considered Group _____.

    A
    B
    I
    R

Buildings containing materials that present a detonation hazard are typically considered _____ occupancies.

    Group H-1

    Group H-2
    D. Group H-5

Please See Answer Key on following page

1 Exam Prep
Florida Building Code-Building, 2017
Answers

Q	A	Section
1.	C	1607.7.3
	D	2113.16(2) – Table
	C	2306.3(3) – Table (d)
4.	A	3306.2
5.	B	454.1.1
6.	B	3306.9
7.	D	3003.1.2
8.	D	3102.8.2
9.	A	1607.8.1
10.	B	1405.14.1
11.	D	1905.1.7(a)

A Fair Housing Accessibility Guidelines – Sect 2/page 3
B 1208.3
A 202 Definitions
B 1805.4.2
A 2902.5
D 3306.7
C 906.1(2)
A 412.5.5
A 2508.5.4
B 911.1.3
A 602.4.3
C 2103.2.4
A 716.5.9.3
D 1809.12
D 904.12.1
B 722.2.1.1 – Table
BE 303.2.1
B 402.5.7.3
D 3002.2
B 1607.4
D 3202.3.4
C 2902.1 – Table
C 2902.1.2
B 1003.2
D 722.2.4 -Table
D 1017.2.2
C 1510.2.1
B 2405.4
C 1709.3.1
C 2304.10.1(26)

Q	A	Section
42.	A	1908.4.1
43.	B	1507.9.7.1
44.	C	Table 506.2
45.	B	805.1.3
46.	C	2111.3
47.	D	903.2.9.2
48.	B	2504.1.1
49.	B	402.8.6
50.	C	2603.4.1.13(1)
51.	A	602.4.4
52.	B	3306.5
53.	A	3002.4
54.	D	302.1, #10
55.	A	1204.1
56.	A	Table 1607.1

B404.2.3 , 1010.1.1
BTable 504.4
D2902.3.2
A1209.2
B3202.2.3
B3103.1.2
DTable 509
D1807.1.6.3(7)
A2512.4
D903.2.3
B1809.4
ATable 1808.8.1
DTable 412.3.1
C713.4
B1405.16.2
D3104.9(3)
C2406.4.3(1)
B907.4.2.1
A2113.2
A803.12
C3202.2.1
BTable 601
D2603.4.1.3
D2303.2
A2610.6
B2207.1
D602.4
B3306.2
D303.3
BTable 707.3.10
B505.2.1

Q	A	Section
88.	B	2303.2
89.	C	311.2
90.	D	Table 2512.6
91.	A	3004.2.2
92.	C	2603.3
93.	D	1405.16
94.	C	803.1.1.
95.	B	705.11.1
96.	D	3307.1
97.	B	1205.2
98.	A	1609.5.3(4)
99.	C	1010.1.9.2
100.	B	1805.3.2
101.	B	107.3.1
102.	B	1405.7
103.	A	2403.5
104.	B	Table 414.5.1
105.	C	2113.10
106.	D	310.6
107.	B	2407.1
108.	B	1907.1
109.	D	105.2
110.	A	2109.3.4.4
111.	A	1810.3.5.2.3
112.	B	102.1
113.	A	104.9.1
114.	A	105.7
115.	A	110.5
116.	D	107.5
117.	A	110.1
118.	C	115.2
119.	C	302.1, #6
120.	A	307.3

1 Exam Prep
Carpentry and Building Construction
Questions and Answers

Questions Set #1

1. _____

    A. Career pathways
    B. Career clusters
    C. Occupation set
    D. Career set

are groups of related occupations.

2. The purpose of _____ is/are to ensure that building are structurally sound and safe from fire and other hazards.

    OSHA
    Stock plans
    Surveys
    Building codes

3. A _____ is a scale drawing showing the size and location of rooms on a given floor.

    A. Stock plan
    Blueprint
    Floor plan
    Schedule

4. Bulkhead is more commonly known as _____?

    Soffit
    Chase
    Cornice
    Eave

In concrete walls how does a cold joint occur?

    Concrete batches are mixed differently
    Fresh concrete poured on top of or next to concrete that has already begun to cure
    Too much air is in the concrete
    D. There is too much moisture in the concrete and the temperature is below 30☐F

What is the measuring system used by the United States?

    Customary
    Metric
    Standard
    Both A and C

7. A scale of _____ is the most often used for drawing houses.

    A. 1/8" = 1'0"
    B. ¼" = 1'0"
    C. ½" = 1'0"
    D. 1/2" = 2'0"

8. A _____ is a large landing at the top of steps.

    Stoop
    Porch
    Deck
    Large –scale landing

What is a tile without glaze called?

    Unglazed
    Unfinished
    Matte
    Bisque

In dealing with wood basics, what is a cambium?

    The rings of the tree that make give it its grain appearance
    Layer of living tissue that produces sapwood
    The fibers of the tree that gives it its hardness
    None of the above

Which of the following is not identified by a softwood board's grade stamp?

    Species
    Moisture content
    Price per lineal ft.
    Mill number

12. The two basic categories of plywood are structural plywood and _____ plywood?

       Hardwood
       Softwood
       Construction
       Engineered

What does OSB stand for?

       Occupational Safety Board
       Optimal-strand board
       Oriented-strand board
       Open-steel beam

14. The _____ is the part of a window that holds the glazing.

       Muntin
       Sash
       Casing
       Mounting flange

15. The _____ is the overall size of the window, including casings.

       A. Nominal dimension
       B. Total window dimension (TWD)
       C. Actual dimension
       D. Unit dimension

16. _____ are written notes that may be arranged in list form.

       Schedules
       Specifications
       Engineering renderings
       Site details

What does the abbreviation MH stand for in estimating?

       Man hours
       Middle-hand
       Materials holding
       Monetary holding

What is another name for overhead?

    Fixed costs
    Indirect costs
    Static costs
    None of the above

In concrete, what is crazing?

    Another name for moist-curing the concrete.
    Whitest crystalline deposits that sometimes appears on the surface of the concrete.
    Appearance of fine cracks that appear in irregular patterns over the surface of the concrete.
    The formation of loose powder on the surface of hardening concrete.

20. A _____ is a test to measure the consistency of concrete.

    A. Slump test
    B. Moisture test
    C. Cube test
    D. Viscosity test

What type of footings are often used on a lot that slopes?

    Pier footings
    Rabbeted footings
    Monolithic footing
    Stepped footings

22. A _____ is a transit that reads horizontal and vertical angles electronically.

    A. Vernier scale
    Theodolite
    Electronic transit level
    Electronic layout device

23. _____ is the process of spreading mortar or cement plaster over the block wall.

    Troweling
    Leveling
    Parging
    Grading

24. A glue laminated beam is often called a _____ .

   Camber
   Spline
   Glulam
   Gambrel

25. The _____ of a door refers to the direction in which a door will swing.

I. Lock face
   Hinge face III.
Hand

   III
   II
   I
   I and II

26. What does 3 ½" represent on a ¼" scale?

   A. 10 feet
   B. 12 feet
   C. 14 feet
   D. 16 feet

27. On a blueprint, lines that terminate with arrows are_____ .

   A. Dimension lines
      Centerlines
      Leader lines
      Break lines

   Which blueprint page shows the building with boundaries?

      Foundation plan
      Plot or site plan
      Floor plan
      Framing plan

   Which blueprint page shows window and door placement?

      Foundation plan
      Plot or site plan
      Framing plan
      Floor plan

Which page of the blueprint shows the external views of the structure?

Elevation
Plot or site plan
Foundation plan
Framing plan

When precise information is needed about a small or complex portion of the building, what would you look for on a plan?

Section views
A detail drawing
Engineering drawings
Mechanical plan

What part of the blueprint designates the brand and model number of a window?

Section views
A detail drawing
Window schedule
Elevation

33. Concrete mixture is made of _____?

Cement II.
Sand III.
Gravel IV.
Water

II and IV
II and III
II, III, & IV
I, II, III & IV

What material impacts the weight of concrete the most?

Silt
Aggregate
Water
None of the above

What is added to concrete to make it set up at a slower rate?

Air-Entraining admixture
Super-Plasticizing admixtures
Retarding admixture
Water-reducing Admixtures

36. Concrete gains most of its strength in the _____ day period after it has been placed.

> 28
> 14
> 7
> 30

In a slump test, the greater the slump the wetter the concrete.

> True
> False

38. To remove air pockets from concrete _____ is performed.

> A. A slump test
> Moist-curing
> Crazing
> Consolidation

How thick is a #5 rebar?

> 3/8"
> 5/8"
> 1/8"
> None of the above

Which tool measures horizontal angles only?

> Level
> Builder's square
> Protractor
> Transit

When laying out a building, what is the starting point from which measurements can be made?

I. Bench mark
   Point of reference III.
Station mark

> II
> I and III
> I and II
> III

If you are laying out a building and all of the diagonals are square, the building is square.

True
False

43. A _____ is a board fastened horizontally to stakes placed to the outside where the corners of the building will be located.

A. Corner board
B. Batter board
C. Starter strip
D. Foundation board

44. _____ is a measure of how well the soil can support the weight of a house.

A. Load capacity
B. Bearing capacity
C. Load resistance
D. None of the above

What is the minimum distance from the point of excavation that batter boards can be placed?

2'
3'
4'
5'

46. In surveying, if rod "A" reads 4' and rod "B" reads 4'6", then _____ .

A. The ground point of "B" is 6" higher than the ground
The ground point of "A" is 6" lower than the ground
The ground point of "A" is 6" higher than the ground
None of the above

What is the formula for estimating concrete in cubic yards?

L X W X D / 12
L X W X D / 27
L X W X D / 26
L X W X D / 24
point of "A".
point of "B".
point of "B".

48. The sides of footings are molded by boards referred to as _____.

      A. Batter boards
      B. Backer board
      C. Haunch boards
      D. Form boards

What type of clip is used to hold foundation wall forms together?

      Snap ties
      Bracket
      6d nails
      Wales

In constructing a stack bond pattern block wall, what additional step is required that is NOT needed with a common bond wall?

      Joints should be tooled smooth to seal them against water seepage
      Joint reinforcement must be added to every third course
      Joint reinforcement must be added to every second course
      Full bedding should be performed

What type of support is used over window and door openings in a concrete block wall?

      Lintel
      Girder
      Collar beam
      Bond beam

52. A standard mortar joint when using concrete block is how wide"?

      1/8"
      ¼"
      3/8"
      5/8"

What is the nominal size of a standard block? Choose the closest answer.

      6" x 6" x 14"
      7" x 8 x 16"
      7" x 7" x 15"
      8" x 8" x 16"

P a g e | 151

54. Mortar should be used within what time period, when the air temperature is 80 □F or higher?

    A. 1.5 hours
    B. 2 hours
    C. 2 1/2 hours
    D. 3 ½ hours

55. A _____
window.
is a horizontal member placed at the bottom of a window opening to support the

    A. Trimmer stud
    B. Rough sill
    C. Cripple stud
      Stool

   The curve or camber on glulam beams should be installed with the curve oriented _____.

    A. Up, toward the ceiling
    B. Underneath, toward the floor
    C. In the direction opposite the fastener
    D. None of the above

57. Lumber shrinks, but, is most troublesome when shrinkage occurs across the _____ of a board.

    Length
    Width
    Height
    None of the above

58. A common defect in lumber where a lengthwise grain separation occurs through the growth ring is known as _____.

    Knot
    Pitch
    Ring Shake
    Torn grain

   The type of wood with lowest resistance to decay?

    Redwood
    Heartwood of bald cypress
    Cedar
    Sapwood of all common native wood

If a sheet of plywood has a 32/16 panel identification index, it may be used as a floor decking with a maximum span of?

32"
16"
2'
None of the above

Plywood that is used for concrete forms must be what minimum grade?

C-D
A-C
B-B
A-B

62. Horizontal members that carry the heaviest load of attached horizontal members are called _____.

Girders
Floor joist
Collar beam
Lally columns

When laying plywood subfloor, what is the spacing between each of the panels?

1/8" on ends and sides
1/4" on ends and sides
5/6" on ends and sides
3/6" on ends and sides

64. The main support under a wood deck is called a _____.

Post
Sill plate
Floor joist
Girder

A built-up girder should have how many inches clearance between the end of the girder and the masonry in a masonry pocket?

1/8"

¼"
1/16"

66. If the run of the standard rafter is 12', what is the run of the king hip? Select closest answer.

  15'
  16'
  17'
  18'

What type of door consists of stiles and rails?

  Flat-panel doors
  Raised panel doors
  Solid-core construction doors
  Sliding doors

What is the standard height of an interior door?

  6'8" or 7'0"
  6'6" or 6'8"
  6'4" or 6'6"
  7'0" or 7'2"

69. The proper war to hang a bifold door is _____.

  A. Install the top track, install the door, the install the bottom track B.
  Install the bottom track first, then fasten the top track to the ceiling
  C. Install the top track first, then fasten the lower track to the floor directly under the top rack. D.
  None of the above

What is the door hinge size for a 1- 3/8" interior door?

  3" x 3 ½"
  2 ½ x 2 ½"
  3" x 3"
  3 ½" x 3 ½"

When installing a door stop, nail the stop on which side first?

  Hinge side first
  Lock side first
  It does not matter which side
  Depends if it is a right or left hand door

When installing plywood soffit to the ledger strip, nails should be installed how far apart?

       2" apart
       4" apart
       6" apart
       8" apart

One square of 235 lb shingles will cover how many square feet and weigh how many lbs?

       100 sq ft, 235 lbs.
       50 sq. ft., 100 lbs
       175 sq. ft., 235 lbs
       200 sq. ft., 200 lbs.

The typical exposure while using roll roofing is how many inches?

       15"
       16"
       17"
       19"

Roll roofing endlaps should be offset by how many inches?

       4"
       6"
       7"
       8"

When using roll roofing, the strip should be nailed so that it overhangs the edge by a minimum of _____ .

       ¼"
       ½"
       1/8"
       3/16"

77. The proper installation of drip edge call for it to be installed _____ .

    A. It is applied to the fascia and under the underlayment at the eaves, but over the underlayment at the rake
    B. It is applied to the sheathing and under the underlayment at the rake, but over the underlayment at the eaves
    C. It is applied to the sheathing and under the underlayment at the eaves, but over the underlayment at the rake
    D. None of the above

How many bundles of shingles are there in a square of roofing?

    Two
    Three
    Four
    Five

When installing shingles, no nails should be placed within how many inches of a valley?

    2"
    4"
    6"
    8"

80. Gutters are fastened to the _____ of a house.

    Soffit
    Roof eave
    Gable end
    Fascia

Splash blocks at the bottom of drain spouts should be at least how long?

    3'
    2'
    1'
    None of the above

What is the minimum overlap for 6" beveled lap siding ?

    1"
    1.25"
    1.5"
    1.75"

83. The ends of siding boards cut during installation should be coated with _____.

    A. Same color paint as the siding
    B. Water repellant
    Rustoleum
    Termite shield

What is the strip nailed to the end of the rafter?

    Starter strip
    Fascia
    Frieze
    Ventilator

What is used at the brick course below the bottom of the sheathing and framing?

    Girders
    Floor joists
    Flashing
    Brick veneer

86. Radiating stair treads are also known as _____ .

    Landings
    Newels
    Risers
    Winders

What is the horizontal length of a stairway called?

    Total run
    Total rise
    Unit rise
    Unit run

The total rise for a stairway is 8'-11". What is the total amount of risers in the stairway?

    13
    14
    15
    16

A stair stringer must have how many inches remaining after it has been notched?

    2"
    2 ½"
    3"
    3 ½"

A third stair stringer should be installed in the middle of the stairs when the stair width exceeds what width?

     2'0"
     2'4"
     2'6"
     2' 8"

How tall is a standard kitchen base cabinet, not including the counter top?

     34"
     34 ½"
     36"
     38"

How deep is a standard kitchen wall cabinet?

     10"
     12"
     14"
     18"

How deep is a standard kitchen base cabinet?

     18"
     20"
     24"
     28"

94. When installing ¾" thick cabinets to studs covered with ½" drywall, how long should the screws be to fasten the cabinets to the wall?

     A. 2 ¼" or long enough to go through the ¾ backrail and wall covering and extend at least 2" into the studs
     B. 2 ¼" or long enough to go through the ¾ backrail and wall covering and extend at least 1" into the studs
     C. 2 1/2" or long enough to go through the ¼ backrail and wall covering and extend at least 1" into the studs
     D. None of the above

A contractor is installing wall cabinets in a new home built with 2 x 6 studs. Some of the cabinets span only a single stud. How are the cabinets attached?

>   With two #10 screws into the single stud and at least two 3/16" x 3 ½" toggle bolts through the drywall.
>   With four #10 screws into the single stud and at least two 3/16" x 3 ½" toggle bolts through the drywall.
>   With two #10 screws into the single stud and at least two 5/16" x 3 ½" toggle bolts through the drywall.
>   None of the above

How long should wood flooring be stored in the building in which it is going to be installed in to allow for acclimation?

>   A. At least 3 days
>   B. At least 4 days
>   C. At least 7 days
>   D. 14 days

The first board of tongue and groove flooring should be installed how many inches from the frame wall and which side of the board should face the wall?

>   1/4" to 5/8", tongue end
>   1/2" to 5/8", tongue end
>   1/2" to 5/8", grooved end
>   1/2" to 3/8", grooved end

What type of product is used as a base for tile and in shower stalls?

>   Backerboard
>   Sheathing
>   Plywood
>   Fiberglass

Which of the following is NOT a common unit of measure?

>   Length
>   Liquid
>   Volume
>   Weight

Cracks in lumber that run parallel to and between the annular rings are called _____

>   crooks
>   cracks
>   shakes
>   splits

A board measures 6' long, 10" wide and 2" thick. How many board feet of lumber are contained in this board?

0
10
1.3
15

Which of the following statements are not true of plywood?

Face and cross band is in the same direction.
There are always an odd number of piles.
Grain in outside layers runs in the same direction.
Grain in successive plies runs at right angles.

The best appearing face veneer' of a softwood plywood panel is indicated by the letter _____

A
B
E
N

Panels made from reconstituted wood bonded with adhesive under heat and pressure are known as

_____

Wafer board
OSB
Hard board
All of the above

Engineered lumber products are designed as replacements or substitutes for: _____

Solid lumber
Second growth lumber
Steel framing
Structural lumber

Laminated veneer lumber is manufactured in lengths up to _____

30 feet.
40 feet.
50 feet.
66 feet

The tool most commonly used to lay out or test angles other than those laid out with squares is called
_____

       a sliding T-bevel
       a compass
       a protractor
       a caliper

The saw commonly used with a miter box is called a _____.

       Cross-saw
       Rip-saw
       Back-saw
       Hack-saw

The size of a claw hammer is determined by _____.

       Length of the claw.
       Overall dimension
       Weight of the entire hammer
       Weight of the head

To bore holes over one inch in diameter, the carpenter uses a (an) _____

       Auger bit
       Bit brace
       Expansion bit
       Hole saw

A _____ cut, is a type of mitre cut that is made through the thickness of a board

       Bevel
       Mitre
       Coping
       Chamfer

A level transit differs from a builders level in that it _____

    A. can traverse a 360 horizontal angle
    B. can measure vertical angles
    C. has a vernier scale
    D. has four leveling screws

A _____ is a mark on a permanent fixed object from which measurements and elevations are taken.

> turning point
> station
> reference
> bench mark

The point of reference where the builder's level is located is called the _____

> Degree mark
> Bench mark
> Elevation mark
> Station mark

Batter boards should be set a minimum of _____ the building lines and in such a manner that they will not be disturbed during excavation and construction.

> 4' outside.
> 4 ' inside.
> 5' outside
> 10' outside

One of the advantages of the balloon frame is that _____

> The bottom plates act as fire stops
> There is little shrinkage in the frame
> The second floor joists rest on a ribbon instead of a plate
> It is stronger, stiffer and more resistant to lateral pressures

A system of framing where the floor joists of each story rest on the top of the plates of the story below _____ is called framing.

> stud
> balloon
> platform
> post and beam

In what type of construction would you usually find "ribbons"?

> Post and beam
> Balloon framing
> Platform Framing
> Any of the above

A large horizontal beam that supports the inner ends of floor joists is called a _____

    Pier
    Girder
    Stud
    Sill

Which of the following is not a commonly available wood beam or girder?

    Solid Wood beam
    Laminate beam
    Glue Laminate
    Built up

121. Ten 2'L x 12"W X 16H" board contain _____ board feet of lumber.

    240
    320
    267
    400

The top and bottom horizontal members of a wall frame are called _____

    headers
    plates
    trimmers
    sills

The horizontal wall member supporting the load over an opening is called a _____

    header
    rough sill
    plate
    truss

When framing a pre-hung door unit that has a 36" door, what would the width of the rough opening be?

    38"
    40"
    the width of the unit plus 1/2"
    the width of the unit plus 1"

A birds mouth is a notch cut in a rafter to fit it to the _____

     fascia
     ridge
     soffit
     plate

A member of the cornice generally fastened to the rafter tails is called the?

     Drip
     Fascia
     Plancher
     Soffit

A window that consists of an upper and lower sash that slides vertically is called a _____

     casement window
     double-hung window
     hopper window
     sliding window

Stairways in residential construction should have a minimum width of _____

     thirty inches
     thirty-two inches
     thirty six inches
     forty inches

Most building codes specify a minimum headroom clearance of _____

     6'6"
     6' 8"
     7'0"
     7'6"

The horizontal part of a step upon which the foot is placed is called the _____

     riser
     nosing
     tread
     baluster

Questions Set #2

1 .Which of the following methods would allow you to determine the location of a proposed building?

    A. Using an instrument such as bench mark
    B. Measuring from an established reference line
    C. Using an optical level
    D. Both B and C

2. _____ drying lumber is stacked in an oven and dried with steam and heat?

        Air
        Oven
        Seasoning
        Kiln

3. A_____ is a metal guide attached to a flat bar, which slips into slots in the front of the saw's shoe?

        Guard
        Baseplate
        Fence
        Motor

What are some patterns of decking or planking in contemporary architecture?

        V-joint
        Eased joint
        Double tongue and groove
        All of the above

The three basic types of ladders are?

        Folding
        Extension
        Straight
        All of the above

There are several careers related to construction. Landscape design, architect and interior design are all opportunities that require knowledge of _____ building construction?

        Craft
        Professional
        Technical
        None of the Above

7. _____ is generally 3/4" thick?

    A. Wood siding
    B. Board siding
    C. Drop Siding
    D. Bevel siding

8. Flakes of wood that are randomly aligned throughout a panel describe _____?

    A. Waferboard
    B. Fiberboard
    C. OSB
    D. Hardboard

9. The standard-size for T & G panels measure on the face _____, with additional allowance for the tongue?

    A. 2' x 6'
    B. 4' x 8'
    C. 5' x 10'
    D. 8' x 8'

What is difference between a hip rafter and a valley rafter?

    Hip rafters extend vertically from the corners formed by plates; valley rafter from the plate
    Hip rafters extend from the corners formed by plates; valley rafters extend from the plate
    Hip rafters extend from the corners formed by plates; valley rafters extend parallel from the plate
    Both B and C

11. There are _____ type(s) of scheduling needed in building a home?

    Two
    Three
    Four
    Five

12. Survey, deed, and abstract of title are considered _____ documents?

    Government
    Loan
    Shipping
    Legal

13. Plastic films, aluminum foil, and asphalt-laminated papers are _____ among the effective materials?

    A. Radiant barriers
    B. Vapor barriers
    C. Insulation barriers
    D. Insulating values

14. On slopes 4 in 12 or steeper, applying an additional course of _____ No. 30 forms

    A. Side locks
       Underlayment
       Eaves flashing
       Center rotation

The best time to provide protection against termites is after construction is complete?

       True
       False

A proportion between two sets of dimensions, as between those of a drawing and its original is defined as a _____ .

    A. Scale
    B. Drawing
    C. Symbol
    D. Blueprint

17. When laying out ceiling joists, the distance between the first two joists will be less than _____ , depending on the center space used?

    A. 2" or 6"
    B. 16" or 24"
    C. 18" or 24"
    D. 20" or 24"

18. A rectangular opening cut with the grain of wood is called a _____ .

    A. Fence
    B. Miter
    C. Bevel
    D. None of the above

19. The most common framing connector is _____ .

    A. Glulam beam
    B. Post base
    C. Joist hanger
    D. Hurricane clips

20. The metal bracket used to attach a shed roof to a building is called a _____ .

    A. Collar tie
    B. Ceiling joist
    C. Saddle brace
    D. Ridge strap

21. The standard size for a single garage door is _____ .

    A. 9' x 61/4' or 7'
    B. 9'/2' x 61/4' or 7'
    C. 9' x 71/4' or 81/4'
    D. 8' x 91/4' or 10'

22. Make sure panel is supported, hold saw at low angle, when cutting on table saw, always place good side face up, and store by laying sheets flat are precautions that must be taken when working with _____ .

    Cedarwood
    Softwoods
    Plywood
    Picea mariana

What type of flashing is used to install a skylight in a tile roof?

    Flexible lead step
    Fiberboard
    Eave
    Metal

What two handsaws are used for cutting irregular curves?

    Back saw and Miter box saw
    Coping saw and Dovetail saw
    Compass saw and Coping saw
    None of the above

How many cuts are necessary to make a rabbet on a table saw with a single saw blade?

    1
    2
    3
    4

26. The run of valley cripple No.13 is _____ the spacing of jacks on center?

    Two-third
    One-fourth
    Half
    Twice

27. The extension of a gable roof beyond the end wall is called the _____ .

    A. Fascia runner
    Soffit
    Fly rafter
    Rake section

What is the purpose of the exterior sidewall in a structure?

    To support the ceiling load
    To support the roof load
    To support floor framing
    To serve as room dividers

29. There are three types of jambs: the two side jambs and _____ .

    A. The wood jamb across the center
    B. The head jamb across the top
    C. The metal jamb across the bottom
    D. The one side jamb

Why is building paper applied between sheathing and siding?

    It prevents the passage of water through the walls
    It prevents the passage of heat through the walls
    It prevents the passage of air through the walls
    It prevents the passage of termites through the walls

31. The total vertical distance from one floor to the next is called _____ .

      A. Total Rise
      B. Total run
         Newel
         Platform

Why is it best to erect the ridge board in its proper position before beginning the installation of the rafters?

         Adjustments cannot be made
         To prevent the roof from swaying
         It will be easier to make adjustments
         None of the above

Corner, sidewall, and roofing are considered scaffold brackets?

         True
         False

Why isn't let-in corner bracing required when plywood wall sheathing is used?

         Plywood-sheathed walls are twice as strong and rigid as a wall sheathed with diagonal boards
         Plywood-sheathed walls are three times as strong and rigid as a wall sheathed with horizontal boards
         Plywood-sheathed walls are twice as strong and rigid as a wall sheathed with parallel boards
         Plywood-sheathed walls are four times as strong and rigid as a wall sheathed with diagonal boards

35. When wood I-beams are used as floor joists, the rim joists can be _____ .

      A. Solid lumber
         Plywood or laminated-veneer
         Wood I-beams
         All of the above

Below what moisture content is wood safe from decay?

         40%
         30%
         20%
         10%

What jobs will carpenters complete while mechanical subcontractors are doing their rough-in work?

     Install exterior doors
     Install exterior windows
     Complete special framing
     All of the above

38. The horizontal face of one step is called the _____ .

     Baluster
     Nosing
     Tread
     Riser

39. A carpenter needs a _____ to determine the kind of rafters that are needed?

     A. Mansard roof
     Pitch
     Roof framing plan
     Slope

Why doesn't the excavator remove the soil for the footing at the same time the soil is removed for the basement?

     Soil is stockpiled for future use
     Soil is not stable enough to prevent caving
     Soil becomes soft when exposed to air or water
     Soil conditions must be tested by checking existing homes constructed nearby

How deep is a kitchen wall cabinet?

     12 inches
     14 inches
     16 inches
     24 inches

The crown on canmber on a glulam must be placed _____ .

     no crown or cambers on glulams
     on bottom
     on its edge
     on top

The actual size of a 2 x 4 is _____.

       1-1/2 x 3-9/16
       1-1/2 x 3-1/2
       1-9/16 x 3-9/16
       2 x 4

A _____ is the vertical board used to enclose the spaces between trends.

       stringer
       nosing
       riser
       trend

Using ¼ inch scale; what does 3-3/4 inches represent?

       14 feet
       15 feet
       16 feet
       3-3/4 inches

How long must screws be to properly fasten a cabinet with a ¾ inch backrail to ½ inch drywall?

       2 inches
       2-1/4 inches
       2-1/2 inches
       3 inches

A cut made across the grain of a board is known as a _____.

       cut-back
       Back-cut
       rip-cut
       cross-cut

The measure of the effectiveness of vapor barrier is known as the _____.

       perm value
       R-value
       MSR rating
       R rating

Plain bevel siding must overlap at least _____ inches.

    2-1/2
    2
    1-1/2
    1

When placing WWM in a concrete slab what location should it be used in?

    in the bottom
    in the middle
    top third
    none of the above

How many board feet are in (48) 2 x 6 x 8's?

    8
    384
    96
    1152

A 32 inch door should have a rough opening of _____.

    34-1/2"
    32-1/2"
    36"
    34"

An 8d common nail is _____ inches long.

    1-1/2
    2
    2-1/2
    3

A stile is most likely found in which type of door?

    Metal
    Solid core
    Hollow core
    Raised panel

_____ is a condition that occurs when wood's moisture content is equal to the inside of the building the product is installed in.

    acclimation
    galvanization
    fiber saturation point
    incorporation

Spacing for plywood used as a sheathing should be _____ inches between each sheet.

    1/8
    1/16
    ¼
    ½

Kitchen base cabinet height is typically _____ inches.

    36
    34-1/2
    35-1/2
    34

A contractor is installing wall cabinets in a home built with 2 x 6 studs, one of the cabinets span only one single stud. How are the cabinets properly attached?

    Two #10 screws into the stud and two 3/16" x 3-1/2" toggle bolts through the sheetrock
    Four #10 screws into each corner
    Four 3/16" x 3-1/2" toggle bolts into each corner with a 3/16" fender washer on each bolt
    Four #10 screws into adjoining cabinets

On which of the following plans would you be able to find the footprint of the building on the lot?

    Framing plan
    Landscape plan
    Site plan
    Roofing plan

How far from the foundation walls are batter boards set?

    2'
    3'
    6'
    4'

What lumber defect is known as a lengthwise grain separation between or through the growth rings?

Cull
Shake
Knot
Check

The fink truss is also known as a _____.

W-truss
K-truss
S-truss
none of the above

What door consists of stiles, panels, and rails?

Bi-fold door
Neither 1, 3 or 4
Raised panel door
Flush panel door

Which of the following panels will provide an excellent base for tile?

EIFS
½ inch CDX
OSB
Backer board

When wood beams are placed inside masonry or concrete pocket, how much clearance is required on top, sides and end of the beam?

3/8"
½"
¾"
1"

Fireblocking is required in walls over _____ feet high.

10
12
14
16

What are the four basic ingredients of Portland concrete?

       Portland mortar, fine aggregate, coarse aggregate and water
       Gravel, lime, sand and water
       Portland cement, fine aggregate, coarse aggregate and water
       Portland cement, lime, sand and gravel

The typical exposure while using roll roofing products is _____ inches.

17
34
30
18

A _____ is used to support a header over a window or door.

King
Trimmer
Cripple
Joist

What board is nailed to the end of a rafter tail?

Gutter work
Fire-blocking
Sheetrock
Fascia

Questions Set #3

The following questions are trade questions not found in the book.

1. To screw gypsum panels to 18 gage steel studs, you should use what type of screw?

2. A mil gage is _____.

3. A contractor is building a 40' x 24' single story house with a 6/12 straight gable roof and 96" from sole plate to top plate. How many 4' x 8' sheets of wall sheathing are required? Do not deduct openings or add waste.

4. What item is not part of an exterior frame wall?

   Where is the base flashing installed when using brick veneer for the outside finish over wood frame walls?

   When installing insulation, how should the vapor barrier be installed?

   What angle does the valley rafter form with the main ridge board in a roof of uniform pitch?

   What is the rafter run for a straight gable roof with a span of 36'?

1 Exam Prep
Carpentry and Building Construction
Answers

<u>**Set #1**</u>

1.	B	Page 6
2.	D	Page 34
3.	C	Page 37
4.	A	Page 460
5.	B	Page 266
6.	C	Page 42
7.	C	Page 44
8.	A	Page 1018
9.	D	Page 990
10.	B	Page 318
11.	C	Page 324
12.	A	Page 338
13.	C	Page 349
14.	B	Page 577
15.	D	Page 586
16.	B	Page 56
17.	A	Table 2-2 page 61
18.	B	Page 64
19.	C	Page 222
20.	A	Page 226
21.	D	Page 259
22.	B	Page 238
23.	C	Page 287
24.	C	Page 360
25.	A	Page 601
26.	C	Page 44

27. A	Page 45
28. B	Page 50
29. D	Page 51
30. A	Page 53
31. B	Page 55
32. C	Page 56
33. D	Page 218
34. B	Page 220
35. C	Page 221
36. A	Page 223
37. B	Page 227
38. D	Page 227
39. B	Page 230
40. A	Page 237
41. C	Page 239
42. A	Page 244
43. B	Page 244
44. B	Page 247
45. C	Page 244/245
46. C	Page 246
47. B	Page 250/266
48. C	Page 258
49. A	Page 265
50. C	Page 277

51. A	Page 287
52. C	Page 275
53. D	Page 275
54. C	Page 279
55. B	Page 434
56. A	Page 361
57. B	Page 323
58. C	Page 326
59. D	Page 329
60. B	Page 341
61. C	Page 341
62. A	Page 396
63. A	Page 421/423
64. D	Page 396
65. B	Page 401
66. C	Page 506
67. B	Page 597
68. A	Page 615
69. C	Page 616
70. D	Page 619
71. B	Page 620
72. C	Page 557
73. A	Page 626
74. C	Page 629
75. B	Page 629
76. A	Page 629
77. C	Page 634
78. B	Page 637
79. C	Page 641
80. D	Page 651

81. A   Page 653

82. A   Page 663

83. B   Page 663

84. B   Page 552

85. C   Page 698

86. D   Page 730

87. A   Page 732

88. C   Page 734, Step- by-

step application

89. D   Page 737

90. C   Page 736

91. B   Page 784

92. B   Page 783

93. C   Page 784

94. B   Page 796

95. A   Page 797

96. B   Page 975

97. C   Page 979

98. A   Page 993

99. B   Page 42

100. C   Page 326

101. B   Page 63

102. A   Page 338

103. A   Page 340

104. B   Page 349

105. A   Page 352

106. D   Page 353

107. A   Page 110

108. C   Page 113

109. D   Page 118

110. A   Page 166

111. A	Page 136	121. B	Page 63
112. B	Page 238	122. B	Page 432
113. D	Page 239	123. A	Page 432
114. D	Page 239	124. A	Page 432
115. A	Page 244	125. D	Page 481
116. B	Page 370	126. B	Page 552
117. B	Page 370	127. B	Page 578
118. B	Page 370	128. C	Page 730
119. B	Page 396	129. B	Page 730
120. A	Page 398	130. C	Page 725

Set #2

1. D	21. B
2. D	22. C
3. C	23. A
4. D	24. C
5. D	25. B
6. B	26. D
7. C	27. D
8. A	28. B
9. B	29. B
10. B	30. C
11. A	31. A
12. D	32. C
13. B	33. A
14. C	34. A
15. B	35. D
16. A	36. B
17. B	37. D
18. D	38. C
19. C	39. C
20. C	40. C

41. A	57. B
42. D	58. A
43. B	59. C
44. C	60. D
45. B	61. B
46. B	62. A
47. D	63. C
48. A	64. D
49. D	65. B
50. B	66. A
51. B	67. C
52. D	68. A
53. C	69. B
54. D	70. D
55. A	
56. A	

Set #3

S-12

Used to verify coating thickness.

How they figure it: 40+40+24+24=128 128 LF / 4LF = 32 pieces Then for the gables:

The 6/12 pitch would give us a gable peak of 72", or 6'.

6' x 24' = 144 sq ft.

144 sq ft / 32 sq ft is 4.5 pieces.

Bridging

Between the sheathing paper and the wood sheathing, extending into the mortar joint at the brick course below the bottom of the sheathing.

To the warm side of the house.

45

18'

BASIC MATH

NUMBERS

In nature, numbers are symbolic representations of real entities, so they are used to represent them. Different types of numbers are used depending on the nature of the quantities that must be represented; for example, using the numbers 1, 2, 3, etc .... to represent whole numbers as the number of cows in a stall or the number of documents that exist in a given file. This group of numbers is called **natural**, as the numbers in this group are used to count things that have a comprehensive nature. This group of natural numbers can be expressed as…

$$N = (1,2,3,4,5, ...)$$

There is yet another set of numbers which are called **integers**. Integers include natural numbers (explained above), zero and negative numbers. Zero is a simple concept; it is the absence of quantity. Negative numbers can be a little counterintuitive, since we are not used to thinking in terms of negatives. But, what if instead of having 20 cows in a barn, all 20 of them die, what if only 10 of them die? Then you would use negative numbers to represent their absence, meaning that you'll use -10 cows and -20 cows. This group of integral numbers can be represented as…

$$Z = (..., -5, -4, -3, -2, -1, 0, 1, 2, 3, 4, 5 ...)$$

There is another large group of numbers which represent parts of a whole, this set is called the **rational** numbers, and a very broad sense one can say that this set represents all the fractions that can be found, although this group comprises all fractions simplified. A rational rational number is one that can be written as a ratio of two whole numbers…

$$Q = \frac{a}{b} \text{, where } b \neq 0$$

In this case there is a restriction that the number b, which is called the **denominator**; it should be different from zero, because if this takes the value of zero it generates something known as a mathematical indetermination, since dividing by zero that does not generate a result with mathematical sense. The number on top (a) is called the **numerator**. The numerator tells the number of parts that are taken from the unit, while the denominator tells the parts into which the units are divided. Analyze the chart below. Start form the 1/8 slice and work your way "up" in a counterclockwise manner. You will notice how the numerator (top number) keeps getting bigger, while the denominator (bottom number) stays the same; this is because the cake is divided into 8 equal slices, and it doesn't matter how many slices you "take", that particular cake will always be divided into 8 slices.

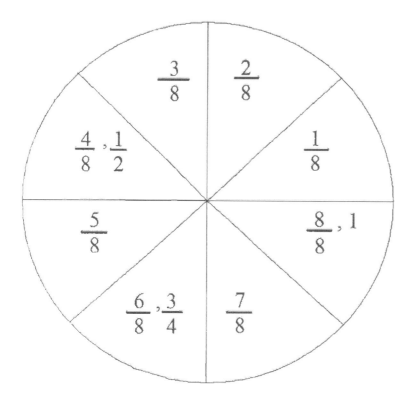

But, wait a minute! What's up with the slices that have two different fractions?, like the one that has 6/8 and 3/4, or the one that has the 8/8 and the 1. This has to do with a process called **simplification**. Anytime we have a fraction, we must try to express it in its simplest equivalent expression, meaning that we will rather say two dollars than eight quarters, even though they are the same.

If we take a fraction like 6/8, and want to simplify it, we must find a number that will divide both the numerator and the denominator (at the same time). In this case the number two will work.

6 divided by 2 = 3 ; and 8 divided by 2 = 4....That is why 6/8 and 3/4 are equivalent.

Greater than and Less than.

How do you know that a fraction is greater or less than any other fraction? Apparently is difficult because one does not know whether to look at the numerator or denominator. But it is useless to look at or compare numerator or denominator of two fractions separately, because they form a single number and therefore should be viewed as a whole. The first rule is to observe that as the denominator is bigger, it means that pieces of the pie are getting smaller. Let's compare the following numbers and determine which one is larger.

$$1 / 3 \text{ and } 1 / 8$$

What do these numbers mean? The answer is that 1 / 3 tells me that the cake is divided into three pieces, and that we take one of those 3 pieces (that's a good slice!), while 1 / 8 tells us that the cake is divided into 8 equal parts and we take one of them. In which case do you take more cake? Obviously the 1 / 3 is a much bigger slice that the 1 / 8, then we can say..

$$\frac{1}{3} > \frac{1}{8}$$

As a practice exercise draw two different pies that represent the relationship between this two fractions.

What is the relationship between rational numbers and decimal numbers?

Any decimal number is the product of the division between the components of a fraction. If you divide the number in the denominator of a fraction results in a decimal number. The issue lies in the type of decimal you get. If we speak of a rational number division will generate a decimal which can be of two forms:

A **finite decimal** $1 / 4 = 1 \div 4 = 0.25$

An **infinite periodic decimal** (digits repeating indefinitely) i.e. $1 / 3 = 1 \div 3 = 0.333 \cdots$
This is true for the case when the number is rational. However, there are special numbers that cannot be expressed as the ratio of two whole numbers. These numbers are called **irrational numbers**, and are numbers like $\sqrt{2}$, π, and e.

$\sqrt{2} = 1.4142135623731 \ldots$

$e = 2.718281828459 \ldots$

$\pi = 3.14159265358979 \ldots$

As you can see these numbers cannot be obtained by dividing two particular numbers. When this happens we say that we have an irrational number…

$$1 \neq a / b$$

OPERATIONS WITH INTEGERS: Remember that integers (whole numbers) do not include decimals or fractions.

Sum of Integers

Two numbers are added in the way the naturally join, the only difference lies in the signs of the numbers, for which there are two special cases:

a. The numbers have the same sign:

If so, add the final and usually put the sign, like this:

$$5 + 4 = 9$$

NOTE: The "+" sign is not placed before the result since it is assumed that is positive number always has an "invisible" "-" sign before it.

$$(-5) + (-4) = -9$$

NOTE: that since they have the same sign and are adding up, you must align the numbers normally and then put the sign "-" before the result. The sign "-" should always be placed before a negative number.

b. The numbers have different signs:

$$(-6) + (3) = -3$$

NOTE that the answer be the difference between the two numbers and will carry the bigger number's sign.

Subtraction of Integers:

When subtracting integers, is best to think of it as an addition with a few changes. The changes are caused by the subtraction sign "-", which changes the sing immediately in front of it...

$$7 - (-3) = ?$$

Following our little formula, we just change the subtraction sign for an addition sign and change the sign immediately after it.

$$7 + 3 = 10$$

Multiplication of Integers

Integers can be multiplied by considering the following common conventions of signs:

$(+) \cdot (+) = (+)$
$(+) \cdot (-) = (-)$
$(-) \times (-) = (-)$
$(-) \times (-) = (+)$

The first step is to carry out a simple multiplication, like we learned a long time ago with the so famous multiplication tables, and then to figure out our sign, we use the conventions mentioned above.......

$$(-5) \times (-7) = (35)$$

$$(-6) \times (8) = (-48)$$

Division of Integers

To divide integers, use the same rule as for multiplication, the sign behave the same way, the only thing that changes is the actual division of the numbers.

$(+) \div (+) = (+)$
$(+) \div (-) = (-)$
$(-) \div (+) = (-)$
$(-) \div (-) = (+)$

$$(-35) \div 7 = (-5)$$
$$(-48) \div (-2) = 24$$

These rules are derived naturally from the relationship between multiplication and division.

OPERATIONS WITH RATIONAL NUMBERS (Fractions)

Sum of Fractions

The sum sound is via the following generalized expression:

$$\frac{a}{b} + \frac{c}{d} = \frac{ad + cb}{bd}$$

Note that ad, and cb actually mean a times d, and c times b.

Also note that at the end of the operation it is necessary to simplify.
Example:

$$\frac{3}{5} + \frac{1}{2} = \frac{(3)(2) + (1)(5)}{10}$$

$$\frac{6 + 5}{10} = \boxed{\frac{11}{10}}$$

Note that in this case, neither the numerator (11) nor the denominator (10) can be divided by the same number, meaning that they cannot be simplified any further. BUT, even though the answer cannot be simplified, it can be written in a different form. It can be written as a **mixed** fraction (numerator is bigger than denominator). This basically means that your pizza only has 10 slices, but you need 11 slices, so you need 1 pizza and a tenth (or slice) of another pizza. Based on this we can conclude that the answer could be written as:

$$1\frac{1}{10}$$

In the event that you have to add more than two fractions, then the associative property of addition can be applied. It indicates that the numbers or fractions can be added in pairs first, and then those results added until one arrives to the final answer.

Subtraction of Fractions

Subtraction is just like addition. The only thing that must be remembered is subtract instead of adding and keep all fraction and number in the same order. This last requisite is especially important, since it is not the same to have 5- 6, than 6-5 (the first one will result in negative (-) 1 and the latter will result in positive (+) 1).

$$\frac{a}{b} - \frac{c}{d} = \frac{ad - cb}{bd}$$

Multiplication of Fractions

Multiplication is by far, the simplest of all fractions' operations. One must simply multiply numerator with numerator and denominator with denominator, or top with top and bottom with bottom.

$$\frac{a}{b} \times \frac{c}{d} = \frac{ac}{bd}$$

Division of Fractions

There are two ways to approach the division of fractions.

$$\frac{a}{b} \div \frac{c}{d} = \frac{\frac{a}{b}}{\frac{c}{d}} = \frac{ad}{bc}$$

OR,

$$\frac{a}{b} \div \frac{c}{d} = \frac{a}{b} \times \frac{d}{c} = \frac{ad}{bc}$$

Example:

$$\frac{2}{5} \div \frac{1}{3} = \frac{\frac{2}{5}}{\frac{1}{3}} = \frac{6}{5}$$

OR,

$$\frac{2}{5} \div \frac{1}{3} = \frac{2}{5} \times \frac{3}{1} = \frac{6}{5}$$

Note that the anwers can be left alone, since it cannot be simplified.

Ratios and Proportions

The **ratio** between two numbers is defined as the quotient (relation) between them, which is symbolized as

$$\frac{a}{b} \quad \text{or} \quad a{:}b$$

Which reads as: " a is to b.."

The ratio is the number that is to relate or compare these quantities. For example, if there are 3 gallons of water per gallon of milk at a particular convenience store, then it can be said that the ratio of water to milk is....

$$\frac{3}{1} \quad \text{Or} \quad 3:1 \quad \text{Or simply} \quad 3$$

A Proportion is a set of two equal ratios, and it is symbolized the following way:

$$\frac{a}{b} = \frac{c}{d}$$

In order for this equality to hold true, then "ad" must equal to "bc". For example, if given the proportion

$$\frac{3}{8} = \frac{9}{24}$$

Then, it can be assumed that $(3)(24) = (8)(9)$, which in fact is true.

Solving for Unknown Variables

Now that we have so much knowledge under our belts, let's try to conquer some of the tough operations in algebra. Suppose you are a contractor running a six-men crew. If you know that each man can erect 25 yards of fence per day; how long would it take your entire crew to complete 1,500 yards of fence?

Step One: Gather data from the problem

1 man = 25 yards per day
6 men = 6 x 25 yards / day = 150 yards per day
Total Length of Fence = 1,500
Total Installation Time = Unknown ?

Step Two: Set up the equation(s)

If in 1 day, 150 yards are erected

Then,

How many days would it take to erect 1,500 yards?

$$\frac{1}{?} = \frac{150}{1500}$$

Step Three: Solve for your Unknown

This step is crucial; this is the part where most students get lost. First of all, since at this point the value we are looking for is obviously not know, we can use any "variable", it can be any letter of symbol you choose (x is commonly used). As soon as the equation is set up, we must leave it by itself on one side of the equal sign. We can accomplish this "working backwards", Lets see,

Since "?" is dividing the number one, we must send it to the other side, across from the equal sign. Anytime this is done, we must perform the "opposite" operation. For example, if the "?" was adding, we would make subtract at the other side, if it was multiplying we would make it divide, and so on. In this case, we must make it multiply on the other side o the equation.

$$1 = ? \times \frac{1}{10} \quad \text{\textit{notice that the fraction has been simplified}}$$

Now, we must send the 1 / 10 to the other side (we must leave the "?" by itself), but instead of multiplying, it will be dividing (do you remember how to divide by a fraction?).

$$\frac{1}{\frac{1}{\frac{1}{10}}} = x$$

Finally, we know that the answer is 10. It will take you fencing crew 10 days to finish the job.

For some students this last problem might have been too simple, it might have been easy to do by just looking at it, than going through so many formulas and steps. That's true; but, following those steps is vital to successfully answering not-so-simple questions during a test.

Percentage

The percentage is a special proportion of any number (percentage) to a hundred. Percentages are very useful for comparing quantities. If a newspaper says that 20% (%, means percent) of all males in the U.S. use tobacco products, that actually means that 1 out of 5 males in the U.S. use tobacco products. Let examine this last example.

20% of males use tobacco products.
What if there were just 5 males in the entire U.S.?

$$5 \times 20\% = ?$$
$$5 \times \frac{20}{100} = \frac{100}{100} = \boxed{1}$$

This means that anytime you see the expression 20%, it can mean, 1 out of 5, 10 out of 50, 20 out of 100, or 200 out of 1000.

What would it mean then, to say that worker A is 25 % more productive than worker B? This would actually mean that if worker A man install 30 square feet of certain tile per hour, then worker B could only install.......? Let's try it!

If worker A is 25% more productive than worker B, then Worker B is only 75% as productive as worker A. Now, we must find out what 75% of 30 is....

We could punch it in the calculator or do it by hand (know how to do it by hand first!)

$$30 \times \frac{75}{100} = \frac{2250}{100} = \boxed{22.50}$$

This answer tells us that 75% of 20 is 22.50, meaning that worker B only installs 22.50 square feet of that certain tile in a hour.

But, what if, using this same information, we want to know how long it would take worker A to install 22.50 square feet of the same tile? That's right... you must find what the 75% of an hour is. In order to find the answer, multiply 60 (sixty minutes in an hour) times 75, and then divide everything by 100, which will equal 45. Your answer, in fact will be 45 minutes; that's how long it takes worker A to install 22.50 square feet of that particular tile.

CONSTRUCTION MATHEMATICS

In the construction industry, it is of upmost importance to quickly and accurately convert measurements from one particular unit to another. This a key factor in good construction-related communication. It wouldn't make much sense to cut a 159 inch long stud; it would definitely sound better if it was called a 13 feet and 3 inches long stud, or simply 13' 3". In the American construction industry, English units (inch, foot, yard) are commonly used, and due to this fact this study guide will only cover this type of units thoroughly. But, it is important to keep the standard system of units in the back of one's mind, since it will pop up frequently; this standard system is the one that use meters and centimeters (it is used in the entire world, and is easier to grasp since all units are factors of 10).

Another important concept that contractors must understand, is the difference not just in units, but in dimensions a well. There are three dimensions we'll focus on: **length, area,** and **volume** (one, two and three dimensions respectively). Each dimension is different and its quantities cannot be compare to another dimensions' quantities. For example, you would not compare 35 lineal feet with 35 square feet, or 35 cubic feet; these are like oranges and apples, they mean different things.

Length

```
12 Inches  =  1 foot
1 Foot     =  12 Inches
1 Yards    =  3 Feet
```

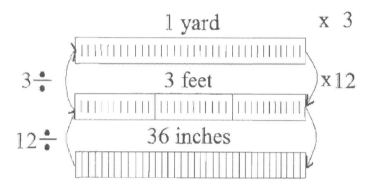

Remember that units of length only have one dimension. Units of length are the measurements from point A to point B.

Area

It is easy for all of us to understand area. This concept is drilled into our heads very often. We normally talk about the square footage of a house or building, the area affected by a particular hurricane, or simply the total area covered by carpet at a particular apartment. Just like in the measurement of length, sometimes is preferable to use smaller or larger units of area depending on the area being measure. For example, it wouldn't be wise to measure the area covered by carpet in square inches, so instead, square yards are use. But, before we jump into learning how to convert from one square unit to the other, we must fir learn how to find different areas.

Area = L x W

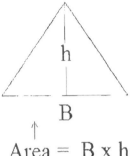

$$Area = \frac{B \times h}{2}$$

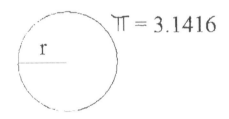

$\pi = 3.1416$

$Area = \pi \times r^2$

Circumference (C) = $2r\pi$

Special Areas

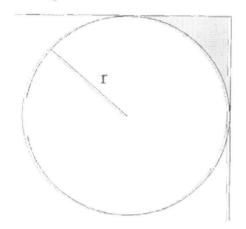

Shaded Area (A),
A = .215 x r x r

Area Conversions

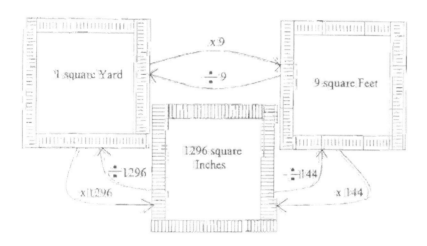

Volumes

Volume measurements are expressed in the form of cubic measurements. That's why you normally hear expression like, "315 cubic yards of concrete were poured today", or "750 cubic feet of dirt were needed to level the road". Things like boxes, concrete slabs, excavations and swimming pools have three dimensions. They all have a length, a width and a depth. When those three measurements are multiplied, the answer is cubic....something(inches, feet, yards, etc..)

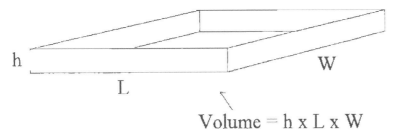

Volume = h x L x W

Note that volume could also be seen as the area times another dimension. Think about it!

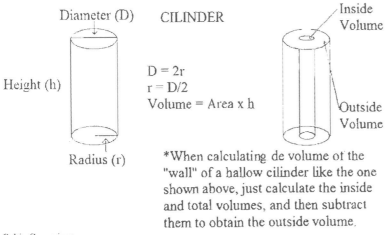

D = 2r
r = D/2
Volume = Area x h

*When calculating de volume of the "wall" of a hallow cilinder like the one shown above, just calculate the inside and total volumes, and then subtract them to obtain the outside volume.

Cubic Cnversions

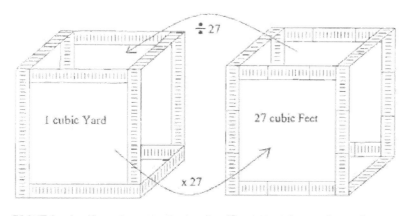

Right Triangles: *No, you're not wasting your time. This concept is key to understanding excavations, batterboards and degree measurements.*

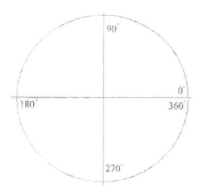

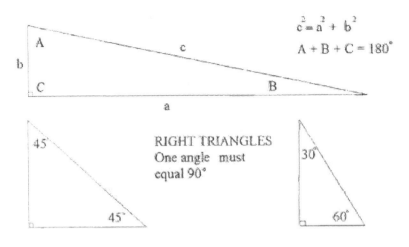

$$c^2 = a^2 + b^2$$
$$A + B + C = 180°$$

RIGHT TRIANGLES
One angle must
equal 90°

Excavations

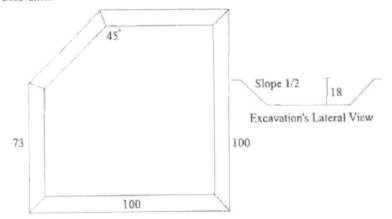

Slope 1/2   18

Excavation's Lateral View

Board Feet

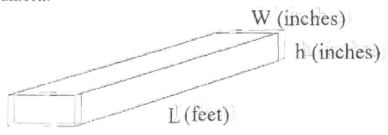

$$\text{Board Feet} = \frac{W \times h \times L}{12}$$

Piles

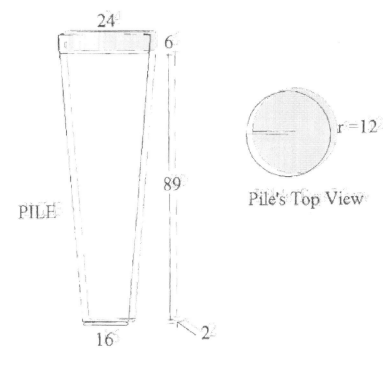

Pile's Top View

Batter Boards

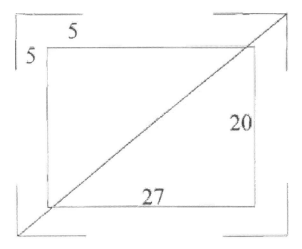

Basic "Roof" Problems: These are called "roof problems", but it does not mean that it is just for Roofing contractors. The concepts involved in solving these problems are essential for any construction field. Concepts like slope are vital for the proper functioning of almost all mechanisms, if you don't think so, ask a plumber or try to drive your truck up a vertical wall. Even though this concepts are helpful for roofers as well, they are very basic for them, and this knowledge alone will not be enough to pass a roofing exam.

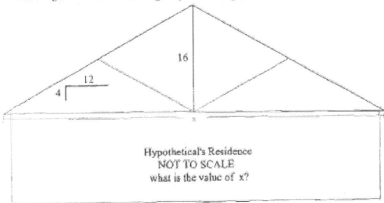

Hypothetical's Residence
NOT TO SCALE
what is the value of x?

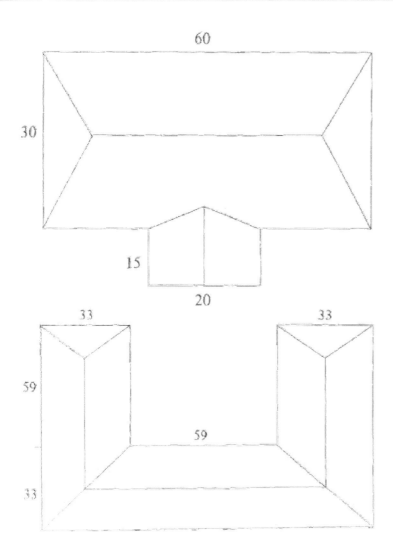

OSHA - 20 Questions & Answers

1 .How many days does the employer have to provide the employee or designated representative access to their medical records or apprise the employee or designated representative requesting the record of the reason for the delay and the earliest date when the record can be made available.

A 24 hours
B 3 business days
C 15 Days 1910.1020(e)(1)(i)
D 7 Calendar days

_____ may only be used to fit test negative pressure air-purifying respirators that must achieve a fit factor of 100 or less.

QNFT
Escape Only Respirators
QLFT 1910.134(f)(6)
SCBA

3. _____ type of respirator is intended for use only for an emergency exit?

A Negative pressure respirator
B Escape only respirators 1910.134(b)
SCBA
Cartridge type respirator

4. When masonry blocks are stacked higher than 6 feet, the stack shall be _____

A tapered back1/2 block per tier 1926.250(2)(b)(7)
B tapered back one Block per tier
C secured with a metallic strap
D secured with a non metallic strap

5. The minimum number of facilities on a jobsite shall be _____ when there are 50 employees working on the jobsite.

A 5 toilet seats
B 10 toilet seats
C 1 toilet seat and 1 urinal
D 2 toilet seats and 2 urinals 1926.51 Table D-1

6. General construction areas shall be lighted to not less than _____ foot candles while any work is in progress.

3
5 1926.56 Table D-3
10
30

7. Portable containers used to dispense drinking water shall _____ .

A be capable of being tightly closed, and equipped with a tap. 1926.51(a)(2)
B be kept less than 90 degrees
C kept off of the ground
D all of the above

An employee shall not be subject to occupational noise exposure of 95 dba for longer than _____ without being administered an effective hearing program.

4 hours 1926.52 Table D-2
5 hours
6 hours
7 hours

9. All personal protective equipment shall be _____.

A new when issued
B have the name of manufacturer
C of safe design and construction for the work to be performed. 1926.95(c)
D A and C only

Employers with _____ or fewer employees and business establishments in certain industry classifications are partially exempt from keeping OSHA injury and illness records.

1
5
10 Partial Exemptions 1904.1
50

11. What is the term for opening and closing a welding tank quickly?

Tapping
Bursting
Planking
Cracking 1926.351(d)1
1926.302(b)(4) Compressed air

12. power actuated tools shall be tested _____

A once per week
B every day 1926.302(e)(2)
C once per week
D before every use

Inside of buildings, cylinders shall be stored in a well-protected, well-ventilated, dry location, at least 20 feet (6.1 m) from highly combustible materials such as oil or excelsior and _____.

A Cylinders should be stored in definitely assigned places away from elevators, stairs, or gangways.
B Assigned storage places shall be located where cylinders will not be knocked over or damaged by passing or falling objects, or subject to tampering by unauthorized persons.
C Cylinders shall not be kept in unventilated enclosures such as lockers and cupboards.
D All of the above 1926.350(a)(11)

Oxygen cylinders in storage shall be separated from fuel-gas cylinders or combustible materials (especially oil or grease), a minimum distance of _____ or by a noncombustible barrier at least _____high having a fire-resistance rating of at least one-half hour

A 5 feet , 20 feet
B 20 feet , 5 feet 1926.350(a)(10)
C 10 feet , 2 feet
D 2 feet , 10 feet

15. Floor stand and bench mounted abrasive wheels, used for external grinding, shall be

A provided with safety guards 1926.303(c)(1)
  bonded
  grounded
  B & C Only

Floor and bench-mounted grinders shall be provided with work rests which are rigidly supported and readily adjustable. Such work rests shall be kept at a distance not to exceed _____ from the surface of the wheel.

A 1/8" 1926.303(C)(2)
  ¼"
  3/8"
  ½"

Adequate precautions shall be taken to prevent employee exposure to atmospheres containing less than _____percent oxygen and other hazardous atmospheres.

  19.5
  20
  20.5
  21

When employees are egressing from trench excavations, A stairway, ladder, ramp or other safe means of egress shall be located in trench excavations that are 4 feet (1.22 m) or more in depth so as to require no more than _____of lateral travel for employees.

  10 feet
  15 feet
  20 feet
  25 feet 1926.651(c)(2)

The employer must notify OSHA Within _____ hours after the in-patient hospitalization of one or more employees or an employee's amputation or an employee's loss of an eye, as a result of a work-related incident, you must report the in-patient hospitalization, amputation, or loss of an eye.

6
8
12
24 1904.39

Air and oxygen cylinders shall be maintained in a fully charged state and shall be recharged when the pressure falls to _____ of the manufacturer's recommended pressure level.

A 90% 1910.134(h)(3)(iii)
75%
50%
25%

21. Electric power operated tools shall either be of the double-insulated type or_____ in accordance with subpart K.

A grounded 1926.302(a)(1)
bonded
ul approved
all of the above

Compressed air shall not be used for cleaning purposes except where reduced to less than _____ and then only with effective chip guarding and personal protective equipment which meets the requirements of Subpart E of this part.

A 30 psi 1926.302(4)
B 50 psi
C 75 psi
D 100 psi

23. An employer must notify OSHA within _____ hours if there has been a fatality of an employee.

2
4
6
8 1926.36

An employer must notify OSHA within 8 hours if there has been a hospitalization of _____ or more employees.

A 1 1926.36
  2
  3
  4

An employer must notify OSHA within _____ hours if there has been an employee's loss of an eye.

8
12
24 1926.36
48

OSHA - 20 Questions

1 .How many days does the employer have to provide the employee or designated representative access to their medical records or apprise the employee or designated representative requesting the record of the reason for the delay and the earliest date when the record can be made available.

A 24 hours
B 3 business days
C 15 Days
D 7 Calendar days

_____ may only be used to fit test negative pressure air-purifying respirators that must achieve a fit factor of 100 or less.

QNFT
Escape Only Respirators
QLFT
SCBA

3. _____ type of respirator is intended for use only for an emergency exit?

A Negative pressure respirator
B Escape only respirators
SCBA
Cartridge type respirator

4. When masonry blocks are stacked higher than 6 feet, the stack shall be _____

A tapered back1/2 block per tier
B tapered back one Block per tier
C secured with a metallic strap
D secured with a non metallic strap

5. The minimum number of facilities on a jobsite shall be _____ when there are 50 employees working on the jobsite.

A 5 toilet seats
B 10 toilet seats
C 1 toilet seat and 1 urinal
D 2 toilet seats and 2 urinals

6. General construction areas shall be lighted to not less than _____ foot candles while any work is in progress.

3
5
10
30

7. Portable containers used to dispense drinking water shall _____ .

A be capable of being tightly closed, and equipped with a tap.
B be kept less than 90 degrees
C kept off of the ground
D all of the above

   An employee shall not be subject to occupational noise exposure of 95 dba for longer than _____ without being administered an effective hearing program.

A 4 hours
B 5 hours
C 6 hours
D 7 hours

9. All personal protective equipment shall be _____.

A new when issued
B have the name of manufacturer
C of safe design and construction for the work to be performed.
D A and C only

   Employers with _____ or fewer employees and business establishments in certain industry classifications are partially exempt from keeping OSHA injury and illness records.

  1
  5
  10 Partial Exemptions
  50

11. What is the term for opening and closing a welding tank quickly?

  Tapping
  Bursting
  Planking
  Cracking

12. Power actuated tools shall be tested _____

A once per week
B every day
C once per week
D before every use

Inside of buildings, cylinders shall be stored in a well-protected, well-ventilated, dry location, at least 20 feet (6.1 m) from highly combustible materials such as oil or excelsior and _____.

A Cylinders should be stored in definitely assigned places away from elevators, stairs, or gangways.
B Assigned storage places shall be located where cylinders will not be knocked over or damaged by passing or falling objects, or subject to tampering by unauthorized persons.
C Cylinders shall not be kept in unventilated enclosures such as lockers and cupboards.
D All of the above

Oxygen cylinders in storage shall be separated from fuel-gas cylinders or combustible materials (especially oil or grease), a minimum distance of _____ or by a noncombustible barrier at least _____ high having a fire-resistance rating of at least one-half hour

A 5 feet , 20 feet
B 20 feet , 5 feet
C 10 feet , 2 feet
D 2 feet , 10 feet

15. Floor stand and bench mounted abrasive wheels, used for external grinding, shall be

A provided with safety guards
  bonded
  grounded
  B & C Only

Floor and bench-mounted grinders shall be provided with work rests which are rigidly supported and readily adjustable. Such work rests shall be kept at a distance not to exceed _____ from the surface of the wheel.

  1/8"
  ¼"
  3/8"
  ½"

Adequate precautions shall be taken to prevent employee exposure to atmospheres containing less than _____percent oxygen and other hazardous atmospheres.

  19.5
  20
  20.5
  21

When employees are egressing from trench excavations, A stairway, ladder, ramp or other safe means of egress shall be located in trench excavations that are 4 feet (1.22 m) or more in depth so as to require no more than _____ of lateral travel for employees.

  10 feet
  15 feet
  20 feet
  25 feet

The employer must notify OSHA Within _____ hours after the in-patient hospitalization of one or more employees or an employee's amputation or an employee's loss of an eye, as a result of a work-related incident, you must report the in-patient hospitalization, amputation, or loss of an eye.

6
8
12
24

Air and oxygen cylinders shall be maintained in a fully charged state and shall be recharged when the pressure falls to _____ of the manufacturer's recommended pressure level.

90%
75%
50%
25%

21. Electric power operated tools shall either be of the double-insulated type or_____ in accordance with subpart K.

grounded
bonded
ul approved
all of the above

Compressed air shall not be used for cleaning purposes except where reduced to less than _____ and then only with effective chip guarding and personal protective equipment which meets the requirements of Subpart E of this part.

A 30 psi
B 50 psi
C 75 psi
D 100 psi

23. An employer must notify OSHA within _____ hours if there has been a fatality of an employee.

2
4
6
8

An employer must notify OSHA within 8 hours if there has been a hospitalization or _____ or more employees.

1
2
3
4

An employer must notify OSHA within _____ hours if there has been an employee's loss of an eye.

8
12
24
48

Made in the USA
Las Vegas, NV
16 November 2023

80935303R00116